Foreword

This book is dedicated to the memory of Marty Chizzick. A great riding buddy.

We would like to thank:
> Robert Urquhart for planting the seed.
> The Gut Grinder group for introducing me (Terry) to many of these routes and
> > keeping the spirit of Horace.
> Esther, Colin & Erica for letting me (Terry) out of the house to ride.
> The City of Boulder Bicycling Program.
> Connie Carpenter-Phinney, & Davis and Damon Phinney for their help.

You may contact the authors with comments, suggestions for the next edition or questions at:

Internet E-Mail AXTF20A@Prodigy.com
or Mail: 736 7th St.
            Boulder, CO 80302-7403

ISBN 0-9646209-0-1
Copyright © 1995 by Terry & Burt Struthers
February 1996 Second Edition

Bicycling has inherent dangers often increased when riding in the proximity of motorized vehicles. All risks are assumed by the reader/rider. Riding conditions, such as traffic volume, vary for many reasons. Riders must evaluate the current conditions before following any routes suggested in this book.

Table of Contents

*Changed from last edition and now out order in distance rank

Introduction

We have attempted to provide a compilation of information that will serve such diverse needs as assisting:

beginning riders to find their way around;

intermediate/recreational cyclists progress into more difficult rides gradually and fully informed as to what they are getting themselves into and have a base for comparison;

serious riders plan a training program;

visiting cyclists target the best routes for their limited time in the area.

This is a difficult objective but we hope you will find the information we have compiled useful.

The authors are a father and son who have lived in Boulder for about 20 years and have been avid cyclists for most of that time. The Boulder area has many special resources to offer the cyclist. We hope you enjoy them as much as we have.

You will notice that there is a concentration of routes in the north and west. The reason for this is the large metropolitan area known as Denver to our southeast and our desire to ride with as little motor vehicle traffic as possible. There is less traffic to the north and west; therefore, in our opinion, the routes are better in that direction. We prefer not driving to get to a bike ride. Sometimes, however, it is the safer choice if you wish to ride a certain route. You will find a few such recommendations.

Organization of Book-We have organized the book into 3 sections:

1) **In Town/Path Rides**, in or near town routes to "get your legs". The map for all of these routes is on one page.

2) **Main Routes**. Routes out of town ranging from 10 to 80 miles. These are the heart of the book. All of these routes include an altitude graph and map. An **area map** showing the location of all the Main and Mega Routes leads off this section.

3) **Mega-routes**, usually a combination of Main Routes and often beyond. These are not mapped but only provided to give ideas for long routes.

Types of Routes Included-All of the main routes are pavement, with two exceptions, and therefore accessible to fat and skinny tires. Each Main Route has fat and skinny tire options. The fat tire routes are usually 2WD gravel or 4WD roads. We have NOT attempted to include single track routes, they are covered in other publications.

Types of Information-As you discovered the first time you pedaled a bicycle, the lay of the land has as much to do with the amount of energy expended on a ride as has the distance traveled. For this reason we have spent much of the time and effort put into this book on the **altitude/distance graphs**. This is the information that is not readily available to riders.

The next page provides a description of our textual layout for each route.

Finally, at the back of the book is a summary of significant laws which pertain to bicyclists. With all that said; go out there and ride to your better health and enjoyment, and please, wear your helmet.

Format Description

Mileage(loop v. out and back): Riding distance to and from start/end point.

Total Altitude Gain: Total climbing on the route.

Steepness: The percentage grade (feet of rise divided by feet of horizontal travel) is calculated for all rides in which the grade exceeds 1% for over 1/4 mile. Both average grade and maximum grade are usually provided. This is highly subjective due to the points at which the measurement is taken but we have attempted to choose those points which best represent the ride for comparative purposes.

Traffic Volume/Existence of Shoulders: This can vary widely depending on time of day, season, and other factors. In our opinion the perfect ride includes no auto traffic and smooth pavement. The perfect ride rarely exists. The inevitable existence of motor vehicles and bumps in the road adds risk of harm to the bicyclist. Therefore, the next best situation is a road with a paved shoulder and minimum traffic. Next down the list of desirability is a low traffic road with no shoulder. We believe the lack of traffic is more important than the existence of a shoulder or smooth pavement. The obvious worst situation is high traffic, poor pavement and no shoulder. The only thing that can worsen the situation would be sharp curves and steep grade (Boulder Canyon). Most cyclists, we believe, share our desire for safety and enjoyment. For that reason you will find our editorial comments scattered throughout the book regarding the avoidance of certain roads even though they may provide the quickest route between two points.

Type/Difficulty: The mileage and altitude will usually do the best job of describing this but sometimes words like 'very difficult' mean more.

Riding Time/Speed Assumption(Without Stops): We have tried to be somewhat conservative but riders will differ in their conditioning.

Start/End Point: This spot is picked for its accessibility to exits from town, and entrance to the direction the route is headed.

Best In Town/Path Ride to the Start: One of the seven routes in the front of the book will be named as the best route to the Start Point as listed above.

Directions: We have indented and provided a symbol: ⌐ to highlight turns for the main routes (as opposed to the options below).

Refueling Possibilities: We prefer a mini-mart or grocery store to a restaurant but the refueling spot may be any one of these. These appear on the map as: (**F**) for FOOD.

Additional Comments: Nothing earth shaking here but significant items or unique observations will be found here.

Skinny Tire Variations: This almost always means paved. If there is a little bit of gravel that can be negotiated, we will mention it. Look on the map for the general location of the options by their letter and number code.

Fat Tire Possibilities: This means gravel. It usually means a gravel road or 4WD road. See other publications if you seek single track. As above, look on the map for the code for a general idea of the location of these options.

Bests and Worsts

Best Rides in the Area (in the humble opinion of the authors)

Best Long Mountain Rides-To Lyons, climb St. Vrain Canyon to Raymond to Peak to Peak Hwy to Ward, descend Left Hand Canyon (Route #23-Option S4). St. Vrain Canyon is a beautiful canyon with low traffic volume-perfect for a sustained climb.
-Jamestown and beyond to Peak to Peak then descend through Ward and Left Hand Canyon to the south or Raymond and St. Vrain Canyon to the north. The short gravel section discourages a lot of traffic but is usually very bikable. (Route #15 Option S1)
-Ward over Lee Hill Rd. then continue up to Brainard Lake if you still need to climb. Route #18.

Best Short Mountain Rides-Flagstaff Mtn. (Route #12). Its close, steep and affords wonderful views of Boulder and the Indian Peaks.
-Sunshine Canyon to the end of the pavement. Less tourist traffic than Flagstaff (so better on weekends) and almost as scenic. Route #9.

Best Long Plains Ride-Carter Lake (Route #20). Probably the quietest corner of the county for a long ride with just enough climbing to keep it interesting.

Best Short Plains Ride-Nelson Rd./75th Loop (Route #13). Close to town, rolling, low traffic volume (once off US 36), and a wonderful descent down Nelson Rd. make this a great ride.

Best Close to Town Classic-The Morgul-Bismark is a rolling ride, somewhat unique for a plains ride. Development in this part of the county has reduced the attractiveness of this ride but it is still a classic. (Route #11).

Best Fat Tire Loops Near Town-Boulder Reservoir via Cottonwood Trail/Sage Trail/Wonderland Lake. Varied but flat on the plains and hills near the foothills. See Route #5 Options F1 & F2.
-Poorman Rd. Loop, a short mountain ride, close to town. Route 9 or 10 Poorman Rd. Fat Tire Option.

Steepest Rides (Mostly Paved)

#1-Lick Skillet Rd.-A 1 mile 800 foot climb for a whopping 15% gravel climb. We believe this to be the steepest public 2WD road in the county. See Route #18 Option F1.

#2-Magnolia Rd.-4 miles with an average grade of 9% with a section at the bottom over 13%. The only problem with this ride is that it is accessible only through Boulder Canyon (see worst roads in county below). The best alternative is to climb Logan Mill Rd.(gravel) in 4-mile Canyon to Sugarloaf, descend to Boulder Canyon and cross over to Magnolia Rd. Route #10 Option F2a.

#3-Flagstaff Rd.-5 miles with an average grade of 7.4% with a section near the top at over 14% grade. Route #12.

#4-Sunshine Canyon-4.5 miles with an average grade of 6.7% with short stretches over 13%. Route #9.

#5-Left Hand Canyon-18 miles of a 4% average but includes a heart breaking 1.5 miles of 10% grade at the top.

#6-Sugarloaf Rd. (paved) and Logan Mill Rd. (gravel) both climb about 4 miles and average between 6 and 7% grades. Both will deposit you at Sugarloaf. See Route #10.

Worst Roads in the County for Cyclists

28th St./US 36 from Boulder toward Denver

Colo. 119 including Canyon Blvd. and Boulder Creek Canyon to Nederland not including the Longmont Diagonal segment.

Colo. 93 from Colo. 128 to Golden

US 36 from Nelson Rd. to Estes Park

Table Mesa Dr. from US 36 to Broadway

Arapahoe Rd. east of 55th and west of 9th St.

In Town/Path Rides

Map of Boulder with Rides Keyed

1. Chautauqua Park
2. NIST to NCAR
3. S. Boulder Creek Trail
4. Wonderland Lake Trail
5. Boulder Reservoir
6. Marshall
7. Boulder Creek Path

City of Boulder with In Town/Path Rides Highlighted and Keyed to Table of Contents

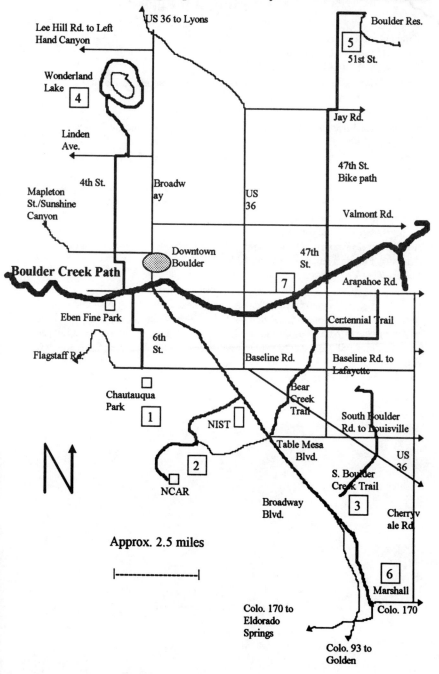

Approx. 2.5 miles

|-------------------|

In Town/Path Rides
1. Chautauqua Park

Mileage(out and back): 3 miles.

Total Altitude Gain: 300 feet.

Steepness: The average grade is 3.8%.

Traffic Volume/Existence of Shoulders: Low traffic on 6th St. No shoulders-parked cars much of the way.

Type/Difficulty: Fairly steep hill. Moderate difficulty.

Riding Time/Speed Assumption (Without Stops): 20 minutes at 9 mph.

Start/End Point: Boulder Creek Path & 6th St.

Directions: Ride south on 6th St. (it jogs to the east) until it dead ends into Baseline Rd.

⌐ *Turn left (east) to Chautauqua Park* entrance on the right (south).

Refueling Possibilities: Delilah's Pretty Good Grocery is about 4 blocks east at College Ave. & 9th St. Chautauqua Dining Hall is open between Memorial Day & Labor Day for breakfast, lunch & dinner.

Additional Comments: Good in-town hill climbing workout. If you want to keep climbing, Flagstaff Road is very available.

Skinny Tire Variations:

S1. Flagstaff Rd. See Flagstaff-Gross Reservoir Route.#12

S2. NCAR. From Chautauqua Park (behind the Dining Hall and to the south of the Auditorium) descend east into the homes along Columbine, Mariposa, Bluebell, or King roads to 20th . Turn right (south) on 20th St. to King Dr. and turn left (east) on King Dr. This will take you to the back entrance of NIST. See the NCAR Route (#2) to continue.

Fat Tire Possibilities: None on dirt.

In Town/Path Rides
2. NCAR

Mileage(out and back): 5 miles
Total Altitude Gain: 750 feet.
Steepness: The average grade is 5.7% with some variability from flat to about 8%.
Traffic Volume/Existence of Shoulders: Usually low traffic. No shoulders.
Type/Difficulty: Fairly steep hill. Moderate difficulty.
Riding Time/Speed Assumption (Without Stops): 30 minutes at 10 mph.
Start/End Point: NIST-S. Broadway & 27th Way on Broadway Bike Path.
Directions: From the front entrance of NIST (National Institute for Science & Technology) ride west around the building on the south side and continue west on Wilson/Lawrence Dr. until you cross Compton Dr. & pass the day care center on the right (north). About 100 yards to the west of the day care, look for a paved trail leading west-southwest. This path leads to homes on Hollyberry Lane.

⌐ *Turn left (south) on Hollyberry* and climb the steep hill to Deer Valley Rd. which cuts back to the southeast. Follow Deer Valley Road up the hill (DO NOT DESCEND Kohler Dr.-stay to the right!) until you see a paved bike path on the right (south) leading over the knoll to the NCAR (National Center for Atmospheric Research) property.

⌐ *Turn right on the NCAR Road* and climb to the top.
Refueling Possibilities: None on the route.
Additional Comments: A great short climb.
Skinny Tire Variations:

S1. Start at Eben Fine Park through Chautauqua Park-Follow the Chautauqua route (#1). Exit Chautauqua at the SE corner of the park behind the playground & follow the paved road down to Columbine St. Descend Columbine to 20th St. Turn right (south) on 20th to King Ave. Turn left (east) on King to the back entrance to NIST. Follow Compton Rd. south to the daycare center on the right (west) & join the main route.

S2. Start at Central Park-Follow the Broadway Bike Path to NIST See Marshall-Route #6.

S3. Start at SE. end of S. Boulder Creek Greenway Trail to NIST (At about 55th & Arapahoe) Ride south under Arapahoe to Old Tale Road just to the west. Ride south on Old Tale Road to its end and cross the pedestrian bridge. Turn right (west) on Centennial Trail. Follow it across 55th and slightly left (south) on to Pennsylvania Ave. Turn right (west) on Pennsylvania. Just past the curve toward the north, turn left (west) on the bike path and follow it over Foothills Highway. Continue straight west for about 100 feet and look for Bear Creek Greenway Trail to turn to the left (south). Follow it to the back end of the Williams Village Dormitories where it joins with the Apache Rd. Path headed left (SE) along US 36 for about 100 feet. At that point Bear Creek Trail continues south under US 36 and finally to the corner of Table Mesa Dr. & Broadway. Cross Broadway to the west and turn north on the Broadway Bike Path/Harvard Rd. to NIST. (3 miles and 140 feet of climbing)

S4. Ascend Table Mesa Dr.-A busy road but more direct for some.
Fat Tire Possibilities: None on dirt.

In Town/Path Rides
3. South Boulder Creek Trail
(Gravel)

Mileage(out and back): 5 miles.

Total Altitude Gain: 120 feet.

Traffic Volume/Existence of Shoulders: This is a trail so no motor vehicles are allowed. Watch for pedestrians and dogs.

Type/Difficulty: Flat gravel. Easy.

Riding Time/Speed Assumption: 45 minutes at 7 mph.

Start/End Point: East side of East Boulder Rec Center between Baseline Rd. & S. Boulder Rd. at about 55th.

Directions: Cross the creek to the east of the Rec Center and

↵ *turn right (south), cross under South Boulder Road* and

↵ *turn right (west) out of the tunnel and* continue southwest under US 36 to the end of the trail.

Refueling Possibilities: East Boulder Rec Center-vending machines.

Additional Comments: A wonderful prairie ride.

Skinny Tire Variations: None on pavement.

Fat Tire Possibilities:

F1. Open Space Operations Center-After crossing under S. Boulder road, turn left and follow the gravel path to near Cherryvale where it turns south along Cherryvale road to the Open Space Operations Center (1.6 miles round trip)

F2. Centennial Trail Access-The S. Boulder Creek trail head can be accessed from Centennial Trail between 55th & the south end of Old Tale Road. From a several hundred yards east of 55th, look for a path leading south. There should be signs indicating Rec center access. This path/route will take you along Meadow Glen out to Baseline Rd. Ride west on Baseline Rd. to Hiawatha. Turn left (south) on Hiawatha to the Rec Center. (1/2 mile one way).

F3. Access from South & West Boulder-Access is available from Thunderbird Dr. on the west side of Foothills Hwy via the pedestrian overpass at Sioux Dr. Follow the bike route signs to East Boulder Community Park and continue east on a bike path to the Rec Center.

In Town/Path Rides
4. Wonderland Lake from Eben Fine Park
(Some gravel if you wish to circle the lake)

Mileage(out and back): 7.4 miles (5.8 miles on pavement)
Total Altitude Gain: 460 feet
Traffic Volume/Existence of Shoulders: Low traffic. Some bike paths.
Type/Difficulty: Rolling. Moderate difficulty.
Riding Time/Speed Assumption (Without Stops): Just under 1 hour at 8 mph.
Start/End Point: Eben Fine Park-W end of Boulder Creek Path, at about Arapahoe & 3rd St.
Directions: From the west end of the park cross north under Canyon Blvd. through the tunnel into Settler's Park. Continue east at the end of the path onto Pearl St. and continue east on Pearl to 4th St.

↵ *Turn left (north)* on 4th. Ride up the hill one block to the end.

↵ *Turn left (west)* 1/2 block

↵ *Turn right on 4th St.* (There is a cut-through from Pearl St. to Spruce St. at about where 3rd St. would be but it can be hard to locate). Continue north on 4th St. to its end at Kalmia. Continue north on the bike path to Linden Dr. Cross Linden,

↵ *Jog right (east) to Wonderland Hill Ave.* and

↵ *Turn left (north).* Follow Wonderland Hill up the short hill to where it curves right (east) and look for a paved bike path on the left (north) in the middle of the curve.

↵ *Turn left on to the path* and follow it up the hill bearing left at the splits. The path continues to the lake just north of Poplar Ave. To circle the lake in a clockwise direction, follow the gravel straight past the west side of the lake then bear right at the split at the northwest corner of the lake. The trail dumps out on to Utica Ave. for a short distance and back to a trail after about 100 feet. Cross the dam headed south and circle back to the west and the starting point of the loop.

Refueling Possibilities: None on the route but the route is never too far from the businesses on Broadway Ave., about 1/2 mile to the east.

Additional Comments: The numerous stop signs on 4th St. may be bothersome to some but the low traffic and nice neighborhood makes it a pleasant ride.

Skinny Tire Variations:

S1. Access to North Broadway. Instead of getting on the bike path off Wonderland Hill, follow Wonderland Hill Ave. east and north to Poplar Ave.. Turn right (east) on Poplar to Broadway. Bike lanes on Broadway will take you north to US 36.

Fat Tire Possibilities

F1. North to US 36 on Foothills Trail and beyond to the Boulder Reservoir. On the west side of Wonderland Lake is a gravel trail which leads north across Lee Hill Rd. and eventually under US 36 just north of the intersection with Broadway ending in a trailhead parking lot. Continuing north and east on the Eagle & Sage trails will lead you to the Boulder Reservoir (See Boulder Reservoir route #5 for more details). It is about 6 miles from Wonderland Lake to the Reservoir via this route.

In Town/Path Rides
5. Boulder Reservoir

Mileage(out and back): 10 miles
Total Altitude Gain: Less than 100 feet
Traffic Volume/Existence of Shoulders: Some bike path, some low traffic, possible high traffic on summer weekends on 51st St. but there is a bike lane.
Type/Difficulty: Pretty flat. Easy.
Riding Time/Speed Assumption (Without Stops): 40 minutes at 12 mph.
Start/End Point: East side of Foothills Hwy/47th St. & Boulder Creek Path
Directions: Ride north on the 47th St. bike path to its end near King's Ridge Blvd. and continue north on 47th St. to Colo. 119 (Longmont Diagonal). Cross Colo. 119 and continue north on 47th St. to Jay Rd.

⌐ *Turn right (east) on Jay Rd.* and ride to 51st St.

⌐ *Turn left (north) on 51st St.* to the reservoir at the end of the pavement on the right.

Refueling Possibilities: There is a gas station on Colo. 119 just to the east of 47th St. The reservoir has concessions in the summertime during limited hours.
Additional Comments: The part of this ride that can be high volume are Jay Road and 51st but there are shoulders and bike lanes.
Skinny Tire Variations:

S1. Nelson Rd./75th Loop-See Main Route #13.

S1a Niwot/Neva Rd./63rd Loop-See Route #13-S3 Option.

S2. Colo. 52-A great plains ride with some hills heading east from this part of town. (See Erie Route #16 or Ft. Lupton Route #19).

Fat Tire Possibilities:

F1. Cottonwood Trail-While riding north along the 47th St. Bike Path past Valmont St., on the right is King's Ridge subdivision/Blvd. Just past the intersection of 47th St. & King's Ridge Blvd.(20 yds.) is a cement bike path leading to the east. Follow it to the northeast until it turns to gravel & becomes Cottonwood Trail. Cross Independence St. and continue to the end of the trail at Jay Rd. Turn left (west) on Jay Rd., cross the Diagonal Hwy and turn right (north) on 51st to the Reservoir. The distance is about the same as the main route but much more scenic and fun. Can be combined with Option F2 (below) for a great loop.

F2. Wonderland Lake/Sage/Eagle Trail Loop- From the Reservoir continue north on 51st on the gravel and turn east at the Trailhead for Eagle Trail (about a mile past the entrance to the Reservoir). Follow the trail to US 36 at the Foothills Trailhead. Continue east on Foothills trail and follow it south across Lee Hill Rd. to Wonderland Lake.(see the Wonderland Lake route #4 to return to the Boulder Creek path.). F1/F2 loop is 18 miles with about 500 feet of climbing.

In Town/Path Rides
6. Marshall via Broadway Bike Path

Mileage(out and back): 10.5 miles
Total Altitude Gain: 330 feet
Traffic Volume/Existence of Shoulders: Most of this is a path but it crosses many busy roads and parking lot entrances. Sections of this are probably the most dangerous bike paths in the city so ride with care. The last section is on a road with very little traffic and no shoulder.
Type/Difficulty: Rolling. Easy except for a couple of short hills.
Riding Time/Speed Assumption (Without Stops): Just over 1 hour at 10 mph.
Start/End Point: Boulder Creek Path in City Park at Arapahoe Rd. & 13th St.
Directions: Ride east on the Boulder Creek Path from City Park, cross under Arapahoe Rd. &:

⅃ *Turn right (south) immediately out of the tunnel.* Follow the paved path up (south) & along Broadway Ave. When on the CU Campus near the Law School (just prior to/north of Baseline Rd.), cross under Broadway to the west side of the road & continue south. The path joins frontage roads such as Sunnyside Lane and Harvard Lane as it continues south. Cross under Broadway again past Darley Ave. to join with Lashley Lane; turn right (south) & continue until the road ends and the path continues. The bike path ends into a road continuing south to Marshall. Stay next to, but not on, Broadway all the way to Marshall

Refueling Possibilities: Many options along the way north of Table Mesa.
Additional Comments: The busy roads and parking lot entrances crossing this path make extreme caution necessary at these points. 360 degrees of very high awareness are necessary at many of these crossings. The traffic declines south of Table Mesa Shopping Center.

Skinny Tire Variations:

    S1. Start from Creek Path & Skunk Creek Greenway Trail (CU Research Park Path)-The Skunk Creek Greenway Trail leaves the Boulder Creek Path near the Arapahoe underpass at about 38th St. Turn south along the trail to the back end of Aurora 7 School. Turn left (northeast) at the T behind the school through some condos and look for Bear Creek Trail on the right (south) before you cross over Foothills Hwy. Follow this trail to the southwest until you join the Apache Rd. Path at US 36. Turn left (south) about 100 feet and cross under US 36. Continue SW on the path to the corner of Table Mesa Blvd. & Broadway Ave. Cross Broadway and join the main route.

    S2. Morgul-Bismark. See Main Route #11.

    S3. Eldorado Springs. See Main Route #8.

Fat Tire Possibilities:

    F1. Community Ditch-See Eldorado Springs Main Route #8-Community Ditch Option F1.

    F2. (Future).South Boulder Creek Trail. There may come a day when this path connects up with the South Boulder Creek Trail (gravel) for a nice fat tire loop.

In Town/Path Rides
7. Boulder Creek Path/S. Boulder Creek Greenway Trail

Mileage(out and back): 17 miles

Total Altitude Gain: 550 feet

Steepness: The average grade on the paved portion of the trail is just over 1%. The average grade of the gravel portion is 2.5%.

Traffic Volume/Existence of Shoulders: No motor vehicles, but occasionally heavy pedestrian and in-line skate traffic.

Type/Difficulty: About as easy as it gets at this altitude and this close to the mountains. The path gets steeper at the west end, particularly the gravel portion.

Riding Time/Speed Assumption (Without Stops): 1 hour 45 minutes at 10 mph. There are speed limits posted ranging from 10 to 25 mph along this path.

Start/End Point: Anywhere along the Path from Colo. 119 (Boulder Canyon) at 4-mile canyon to Arapahoe Rd. near Cherryvale.

Directions: The path generally runs within a block north or south of Arapahoe Rd. from the foothills to east of 55th St. When riding east, bear right at the pond about a tenth of a mile past the 55th St. underpass to make the connection with the South Boulder Creek Greenway Trail or bear left to come out on Valmont Rd.

Refueling Possibilities: Many in-town stores & restaurants are close.

Additional Comments: At the west end about 1 mile above (west of) Eben Fine Park the path turns to gravel.

Skinny Tire Variations:

S1. Paved portion only. The round trip is 14 miles with 350 feet of climbing.

S1a. Eben Fine Park to 55th. Round trip is 9 miles with 200 feet of climbing. From 55th to the east end at Arapahoe-add 1.3 miles one way (almost flat). Eben Fine Park to end of pavement at west end-add 1.2 miles one way and 150 feet of climbing. From the end of pavement at the west end to 4-mile canyon 1.5 miles one way with 200 feet of climbing.

S2. Centennial Trail Loop. At Arapahoe & approx. Cherryvale, cross under Arapahoe & proceed to the end of the path at Old Tale Rd. Turn left (south) on Old Tale Rd. to the end and join the bike path as it crosses the creek toward the south. Turn right (west) shortly after the bridge & continue to 55th St. Turn left (south) on 55th to Pennsylvania Ave. Turn right (west) on Pennsylvania & continue west until the road curves to the north at which point a bike path exits on the left (west). Follow that over the Foothills Hwy pedestrian bridge & continue west, bearing right at the splits in the path through the multi-unit housing. At the back of the school yard (Aurora 7) turn right over the bridge. Continue until you reach the Skunk Creek Greenway Trail-the north/south bike path leading under Colorado Blvd. & through the CU Research Center. Take that bike path north until you reach the Creek Path again at about Arapahoe Rd. & 38th St. This adds just less than 1/2 mile to the out & back route on the Creek Path.

Fat Tire Possibilities:

F1. South Boulder Creek Trail. See Route #3.

Main Routes
(Each Route includes a Map, Altitude Graph and Fat &
Skinny Tire Variations

8. Eldorado Springs
9. Sunshine Canyon
10. Salina via 4-mile Canyon
11. Morgul-Bismark
12. Flagstaff/Gross Reservoir
13. Nelson Rd./75th Loop
14. Peak to Peak Hwy
15. Jamestown
16. Erie Loop
17. Lyons avoiding US 36
18. Ward via Left Hand Canyon
19. Ft. Lupton/East of I-25/Denver/Greeley Options
20. Carter Lake/Loveland Option
21. Pinecliffe via Coal Creek Canyon
22. Golden Gate Park/West Denver Option
23. Allenspark via St. Vrain Canyon

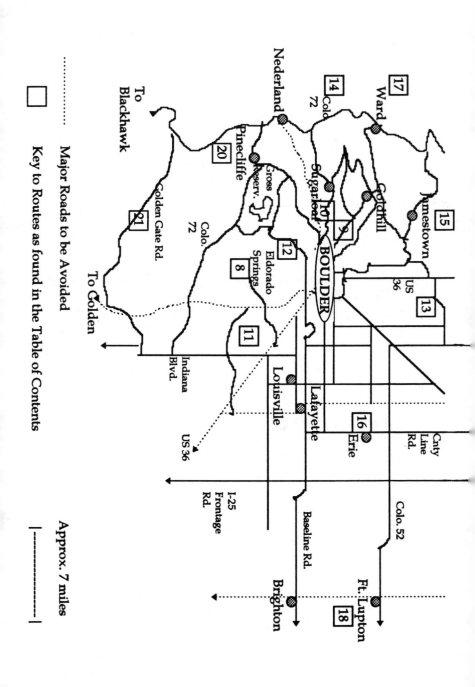

Major Roads to be Avoided

Key to Routes as found in the Table of Contents

Approx. 7 miles

|———————|

15

Area Map with Route Locations
For all Main & Mega Routes

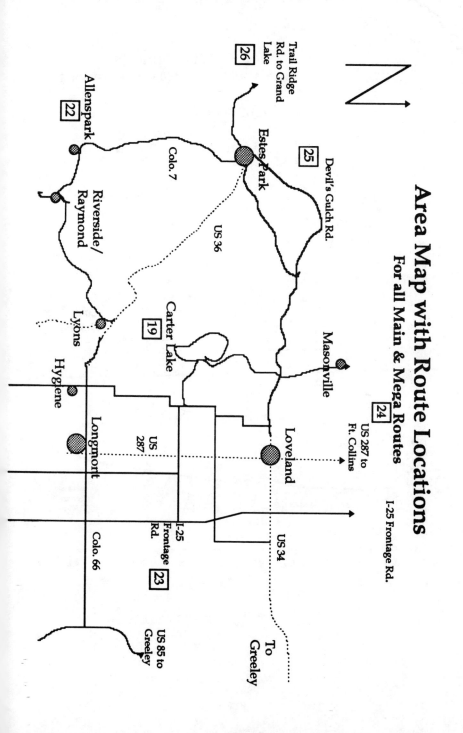

N

Trail Ridge
Rd. to Grand
Lake

26

Allenspark

22

Colo. 7

Riverside/
Raymond

Estes Park

25

Devil's Gulch Rd.

US 36

Lyons

Carter Lake

19

Hygene

Longmont

US
287

Masonville

24

US 287 to
Ft. Collins

I-25 Frontage Rd.

Loveland

US 34

I-25
Frontage
Rd.

23

Colo. 66

US 85 to
Greeley

To
Greeley

Eldorado Springs
10 miles out & back-460 feet of climbing

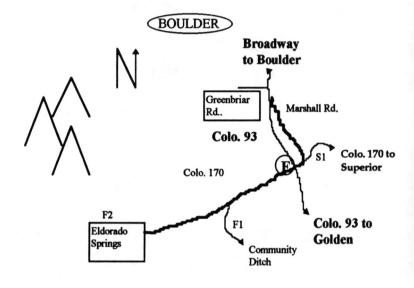

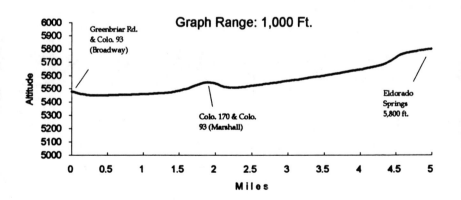

Main Route
8. ELDORADO SPRINGS

Mileage(out and back): 10 Miles

Total Altitude Gain: 460 Feet

Steepness: The average grade from US 36 to Eldorado Springs is less than 2% but there is a .3 mile section that is almost 4% riding into town.

Traffic Volume/Existence of Shoulders: 2 parallel routes are possible. The first, out the end of the bike path and onto S. Marshall Road at the south end of Broadway, affords little traffic until Marshall; then moderate traffic with a narrow shoulder on Colo. 170 out to the park. The second choice is to ride on Colo. 93. The traffic is heavy but the shoulder is wide.

Type/Difficulty: Mostly flat or slightly rolling. Easy.

Riding Time/Speed Assumption (Without Stops): 40 minutes at 15 mph.

Start/End Point: Corner of Greenbriar Rd. and Broadway, at the south end of Broadway as it is about to change into Colo. 93.

Best In Town/Path Ride to the Start: Marshall Route #6.

Directions: Ride south either on the bike path which turns into S. Marshall Road just south of Broadway, or along Broadway/Colo. 93 to Colo. 170 (Marshall). (1.9 m.)

⌐ *Turn right (west) at Colo. 170* at the first stop light south of Boulder and continue west to the end. If you have chosen the bike path you must turn right at the stop sign in the group of houses in Marshall, and you will find yourself out on Colo. 170. Then continue straight southwest until you cross Colo. 93 at the light, then continue west to the end. (3.1 m.)

Refueling Possibilities: There is a gas/snack shop at the stop light on the corner of Colo. 93 and Colo. 170. There is a spring in Eldorado Springs just across the bridge. Donations are requested.

Additional Comments: Once in Eldorado Springs you can watch the climbers or swim in the pool (in season).

Skinny Tire Variations:

    <u>S1. Morgul-Bismark</u>-The Morgul-Bismark passes through Marshall. Please see Main Route #6.

Fat Tire Possibilities:

    <u>F1. Community Ditch</u>. At the point the Mesa Trail ends into Colo. 170 about 2 miles west of Colo. 93 there is a parking lot on either side of the road. Turn left and ride through the south parking lot onto the trail which starts paved to a picnic grounds (.4 m) and up to a 2-track road that follows the Community Ditch, an irrigation ditch, to the east. It crosses Colo. 93 at mile 2.5 and continues up over the white rocks on the east side of Colo. 93 and out to Marshall Lake at mile 4.

    <u>F1a. South to Colo. 128</u>. From Community Ditch at Colo. 93 just to the south of the trail, about 25 yards to the south of the white rocks mentioned above, another two track leads SE and up the hill. At .2 mile there is a trail which leads back down to the Community Ditch trail. The main two-track continues up and over the hill and ends at Colo. 128 (about 1/4 mile east of Colo. 93) at a marked trailhead with a parking lot.

    <u>F2. Continue into State Park</u>. At the end of the main route, a gravel road continues west into the state park for about a mile. A fee is collected at the gate.

Sunshine Canyon
12 miles up & back-1,940 feet of climbing

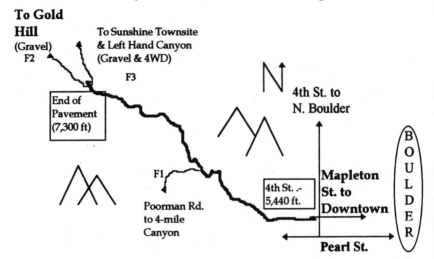

To Gold Hill
(Gravel)
F2

To Sunshine Townsite
& Left Hand Canyon
(Gravel & 4WD)

F3

End of Pavement (7,300 ft)

4th St. to N. Boulder

F1

Poorman Rd. to 4-mile Canyon

4th St. - 5,440 ft.

Mapleton St. to Downtown

Pearl St.

BOULDER

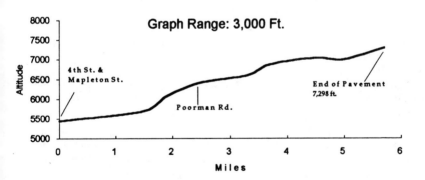

Graph Range: 3,000 Ft.

4th St. & Mapleton St.

Poorman Rd.

End of Pavement 7,298 ft.

Altitude

Miles

Main Route
9. SUNSHINE CANYON

Mileage(out and back): 12 Miles
Total Altitude Gain: 1,940 Feet
Steepness: The average grade from 4th St. to the first small descent (4.5 miles) is 6.7% but the grade varies up to about 14% for small stretches.
Traffic Volume/Existence of Shoulders: Low traffic with no shoulders.
Type/Difficulty: Steep mountain climb. Difficult.
Riding Time/Speed Assumption (Without stops): Just over 1 hour at 11 mph.
Start/End Point: West end of Mapleton Boulevard at 4th St.
Best In Town/Path Ride to the Start: From the west end of the Creek Path, the start of the Wonderland Lake ride (Route #4) will get you to the corner of 4th & Mapleton.
Directions: Ride west up the canyon until you run out of pavement.
Refueling Possibilities: None.
Additional Comments: A nice and less traveled alternative to Flagstaff for a short, steep, close to town ride.
Skinny Tire Variations: None on pavement.
Fat Tire Possibilities:

    F1. Poorman Road Loop. At mile 2.5 turn left (southwest) onto Poorman Road (gravel 2WD) After about 1.5 miles this deposits you in 4-mile Canyon. Turn left, descend about 1.5 mile to Boulder Canyon (Colo. 119) to the bike path on the south side of the intersection. Follow this down to town. Turn left (north) at the Settlers Park underpass of Canyon Blvd. when entering Eben Fine Park. This puts you at the west end of Pearl Ave. Turn left (east) on Pearl to 4th St.. Turn left (north) and follow 4th St. to Mapleton to complete the loop. (10 miles, 1,000 ft of climbing, about 1 hour).

    F2. Gold Hill/Salina Loop. Continue past the end of the pavement from the end of the main route to Gold Hill-3 miles. Turn left in Gold Hill at the first intersection (Gold Run Rd.) to Salina (4 miles) into 4-mile Canyon and continue to Boulder Canyon. Cross Colo. 119 onto the bike path for the short descent into Boulder and the west end of Boulder Bike Creek path. (See F1 for the return to Route start)-22 mile loop with about 3,000 feet of climbing.

    F2a. Gold Hill/Sunset Continue straight west through Gold Hill (see F2) to the Little Switzerland Trail (2.5 miles from Gold Hill). Turn left at the sign and follow the 2 track road down into the town of Sunset in 4-Mile Canyon (4 Miles). Turn left at the road end and continue down to Salina (5 miles). From Salina you can descend to Boulder or turn left in Salina and climb back up to Gold Hill. (30 mile loop if return to Boulder via 4-Mile canyon with about 3,300 feet of climbing).

    F2b. Gold Hill/Peak to Peak Hwy Continue straight past the Switzerland Trail (see F2a) 2 miles to the split in the road. The right fork takes you 1.2 miles down into Left Hand Canyon about 1.5 miles below Ward. The left fork will take you 3 miles out to Peak to Peak highway about 4 miles south of Ward.

    F2c. Gold Hill/Left Hand Canyon Turn right in Gold Hill on Lick Skillet Road at the east end of town. This will take you just over 1 mile and 800 feet down into Left Hand Canyon about 11 miles up the canyon from US 36 and 7 miles below Ward.

F3. Sunshine Townsite & Left Hand Canyon @ Rowena At the end of the pavement turn right (north) and follow the gravel road staying to the uphill/northern splits. The road will eventually peak out at Sunshine Saddle. The 4WD road down to the left (NW) leads down to Left Hand Canyon and Rowena.

4-mile Canyon to Salina
13 miles up and back-1,200 feet of climbing

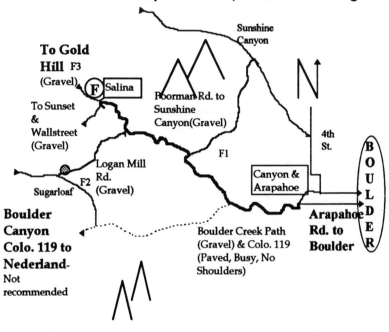

Sunshine Canyon

To Gold Hill F3 (Gravel)

(F) Salina

To Sunset & Wallstreet (Gravel)

Poorman Rd. to Sunshine Canyon(Gravel)

Logan Mill Rd. (Gravel)

F2

Sugarloaf

F1

4th St.

Canyon & Arapahoe

BOULDER

Boulder Canyon Colo. 119 to Nederland- Not recommended

Boulder Creek Path (Gravel) & Colo. 119 (Paved, Busy, No Shoulders)

Arapahoe Rd. to Boulder

Graph Range: 2,000 Ft.

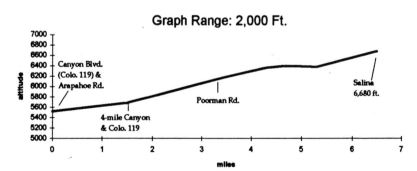

Canyon Blvd. (Colo. 119) & Arapahoe Rd.

4-mile Canyon & Colo. 119

Poorman Rd.

Salina 6,680 ft.

altitude

7000
6800
6600
6400
6200
6000
5800
5600
5400
5200
5000

0   1   2   3   4   5   6   7

miles

Main Route
10. Salina via 4-mile Canyon

Mileage(out and back): 13 miles.

Total Altitude Gain: 1,200 feet

Steepness: The average grade from the entrance to 4-mile Canyon to Salina, excluding the downhill portion, is 4.6% and fairly consistent.

Traffic Volume/Existence of Shoulders: Low traffic volume, no shoulders.

Type/Difficulty: Steady climb. Difficult.

Riding Time/Speed Assumption (Without Stops): Just over 1 hour at 12 mph.

Start/End Point: Arapahoe Rd. & Canyon Blvd. (Colo. 119) on the Creek Path.

Best In Town/Path Ride to the Start: West end of Creek Path (Route #7).

Directions: This is the only ride in the book that starts out on gravel. We recommend the Creek Path as the best route to start this ride. After about 1/2 mile, the path turns to gravel. It can usually be ridden with skinny tires, depending on the time of year and amount of recent precipitation. If you really hate gravel or the path is simply impassable on skinny tires, Colo. 119 can be ridden for the first 1.5 miles but traffic can be very heavy and shoulder width is erratic. In either case,

⌐ *turn right (north) at 4-mile Canyon* and follow it to Salina.

Refueling Possibilities: There is a campground just north of Colo. 119 in the canyon with soda machines and a small store. In Salina (right at the fork in town, toward Gold Hill) is a restaurant on the left about 1/4 mile past the split.

Additional Comments: Probably best on fat tires due to the traffic on Colo. 119 and the gravel Creek Path but also because there are lots of great fat tire options for loops from this canyon.

Skinny Tire Variations: None on pavement.

Fat Tire Possibilities:

F1. Poorman Road Loop. Turn right onto Poorman Road (gravel 2WD) at mile 3.4 from the start of the route. This climbs about 1.5 miles to Sunshine Canyon. Turn right when you hit pavement (Sunshine Canyon) and descend to 4th St. Turn right on 4th St. to Pearl St. and turn right again on Pearl St. to the bike path that splits off to the right through Settlers Park under Canyon Blvd., and back onto the Creek Path at Eben Fine Park.(10 miles, 1,000 ft of climbing, about 1 hour)

F2. Logan Mill Road-Sugarloaf-Sunset Loop Turn left onto Logan Mill Road at the bottom of the short descent at mile 5.4. This climbs sharply to the top of a ridge just to the east of Sugarloaf Mtn. There are many side roads on the trip up. Bear right & up if in doubt, but mainly follow the most traveled route. Since there are no road signs, this road can be confusing, so count on making a couple of wrong turns. The climb is about 4 miles and 1,300 feet (a grade of over 6%). From the top of the ridge, work south/southwest and downhill through the homes about 2 miles until you reach pavement. This is Sugarloaf Road. Turn right and climb the steep pavement about 2 miles and 1,000 feet to Sugar Loaf Mountain Rd and the signs to Switzerland Trail and Sunset. Turn right (north) on Sugar Loaf Mtn. Rd.. This climbs 400 feet and about 1 mile to the top of the Switzerland Trail. Descend the 4WD Switzerland Trail 3 miles to Sunset; turn right (east) and descend 4-mile Canyon about 6 miles back through Salina. (This loop adds about 16 miles and 2,400 feet of climbing to the main route.)

F2a. Logan Mill/Boulder Canyon/Magnolia Road/Gross Reservoir Loop-
Follow the F2 route above until you reach Sugarloaf Rd. Turn left (east), down the road
about 4 miles to Colo. 119 (a grade of close to 7%). Turn left & descend about 1/4 mile
to Magnolia Rd. Turn right (south) on Magnolia Rd. & climb one of the most sustained
steep stretches of pavement in the county-2,000 feet in 4 miles (an average grade of 9%
with a section at the bottom at 13%). Continue past the end of the pavement about 1.5
miles to Rd. 68 on the left (east). Turn east on Rd. 68 and follow the road east about 2.5
miles until the road deteriorates to a 4WD road for about a mile. After a downhill
section it will begin to improve & in another mile you will have pavement and Gross
Reservoir on your right (south). Continue on this road down Flagstaff to 6th St. Turn
left (north) & descend to the Creek Path. Turn west to Eben Fine Park. Total loop is 38
miles & 5,500 feet of climbing. About 5 hours at 8 mph.

F3. Gold Hill-Switzerland Trail-Sunset Loop Bear right at the split in Salina
and climb about 4 miles to Gold Hill. Turn left in Gold Hill on Gold Hill Rd. (52 Rd.)
and climb about 3 miles to the Switzerland Trailhead. Turn left (south) and descend the
Switzerland Trail about 4 miles to Sunset. Turn left (east) on 4-mile Canyon Rd. (118
Rd.) and descend just over 5 miles back to Salina. This adds about 16 miles and 2,000
feet to the main route.

F3a. Gold Hill-Sunshine Canyon Loop See Sunshine Canyon Route #9 Option
F2.

Morgul-Bismarck
13.2 mile loop-1,000 feet of climbing

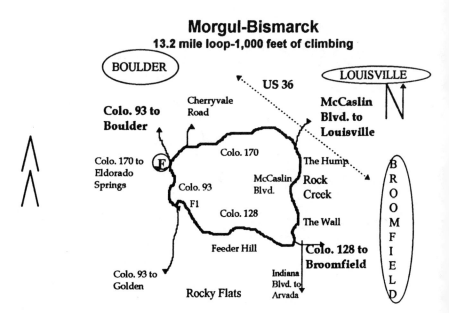

BOULDER

LOUISVILLE

US 36

Colo. 93 to Boulder

Cherryvale Road

McCaslin Blvd. to Louisville

Colo. 170 to Eldorado Springs

F

Colo. 170

The Hump

B R O O M F I E L D

Colo. 93

McCaslin Blvd.

Rock Creek

F1

Colo. 128

The Wall

Feeder Hill

Colo. 128 to Broomfield

Colo. 93 to Golden

Indiana Blvd. to Arvada

Rocky Flats

Graph Range 1,000 Ft.

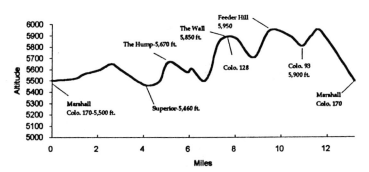

Main Route
11. MORGUL-BISMARK

Mileage(loop): 13.2 Miles
Total Altitude Gain: 1,000 Feet
Steepness: The three critical hills on this route are the Hump just out of Superior-8% grade, the Wall approaching Colo. 128 on McCaslin Blvd.-12% grade and the Feeder Hill on Colo. 128 at a 6.5% grade. The descent down Colo. 93 is 5.7%. All are shorter than a mile.
Traffic Volume/Existence of Shoulders: Generally low volume, except on Colo. 93 and Superior to the entrance to Rock Creek. Approximately 1/3 of route has shoulders.
Type/Difficulty: Rolling, medium to high difficulty.
Riding Time/Speed Assumption (Without Stops): 45 minutes at 17.5 mph. I (Terry) am happy with anything under 40 minutes (it gets tougher every year) which is an average speed of 20 mph. The record time for 7 laps by the pros was 3 hours and 30 minutes by Alexi Grewal. That is an average speed of 26.4 mph and a lap time of just over 30 minutes.
Commentary: A classic ride and great training route. Traffic in this part of the county from recent development and new traffic lights have reduced the attractiveness of this route.
Historical Notes: This ride was an integral part of the Red Zinger/Coors Classic Bicycle Race. It was won by American men only 4 times in 10 years. The men rode the loop 8 times and the women 4 times. Connie Carpenter-Phinney won the race 4 times.
Start/End Point: Town of Marshall, about 2 miles south of Boulder just off of Colo. 93 on Colo. 170.
Best In Town/Path Ride to the Start: Marshall Route #6.
Directions: The best routes out of town to the NW corner of the loop (Marshall) are: 1) Take Broadway/Colo. 93 south to Eldorado Springs/Marshall/Colo. 170 intersection and turn left. You may ride the bike path/side road or on Broadway/93. 2) Take Cherryvale Road south until it dead ends into Marshall Road/Colo. 170.

The route itself is usually traveled in a clockwise loop. This affords all right-hand turns. From Marshall, therefore, ride east on Colo. 170, a gradual rise to the curve at US 36 toward the south to McCaslin Blvd. (3.8 m.)

⌐ *Turn right (southwest) at the road end stop sign at McCaslin Boulevard.* The first hill is known as the Hump. After a short descent and gradual climb the Wall will loom above you. This is the steepest section of the route. At the top of the Wall will be Colo. 128 (3.5 m.)

⌐ *Turn right (west) on Colo. 128.* This short stretch is the flattest portion of the ride. Descend to the bottom of the draw and then climb the Feeding Hill. Continue to Colo. 93. (4.0 m)

⌐ *Turn right (north) on Colo. 93.* After a short climb, descend quickly to the light at Colo. 170. (1.9 m.)

⌐ *Turn right (east) on Colo. 170 to repeat or return to Cherryvale Road.*
Refueling Possibilities: Mile 0-The gas station at the northwest corner of Colo. 170 and Colo. 93 has plenty to eat and drink.

Additional Comments: This route was named after a cat and a dog. Very few access roads coming in to the route make it safe . Very hard work on windy or hot, sunny days due to lack of cover. Traffic can be heavy near Rock Creek entrance and on Colo. 93. **Skinny Tire Variations**: Do it in reverse, maybe? How about 5 times around? 10?

S1. Dillon Road. At the corner of Colo. 170 and McCaslin Blvd. (the Superior interchange at US 36) ride east across the US 36 bridge and after 100 yards past the bridge turn right (southeast) on Dillon Road. Ride east as far as I-25 and beyond. See Main Route #19-Fort Lupton/I-25 for more possibilities at that point.

S2. Golden Gate Park/West Denver. See Main Route #22.

Fat Tire Possibilities:

F1. Community Ditch. There is a trail head on Colo. 128 about 1/4 mile east of Colo. 93 (see F1a Eldorado Springs route #8).

Gross Reservoir via Flagstaff Road
19 miles up & back and 3,200 feet of climbing

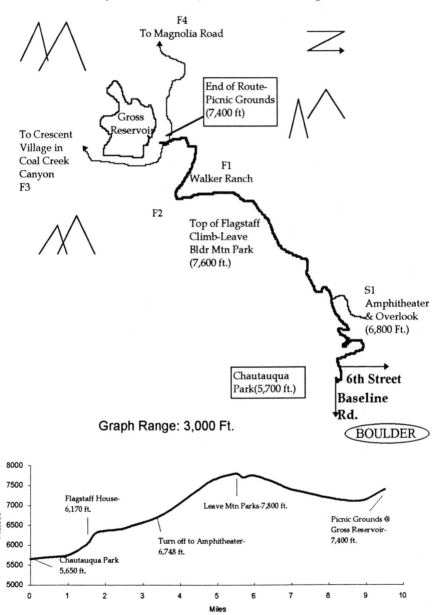

Graph Range: 3,000 Ft.

Main Route
12. FLAGSTAFF/GROSS RESERVOIR

Mileage(out and back): 19 Miles
Total Altitude Gain: 3,200 Feet
Steepness: The average grade from Gregory Creek Canyon to the exit from the mountain park (the "top" of the sustained climb-5 miles) is 7.4%. The grade varies from almost flat (very short) to 14% for .3 mile just below Lost Gulch Overlook. The first 1/2 mile above Gregory Creek averages 10%. The 'bottom half' (3.5 miles)-Gregory Creek to the Amphitheater turnoff averages 6.5% and the 'top half' (2 miles)-Amphitheater turnoff to the exit from the mountain parks-averages 10%.
Traffic Volume/Existence of Shoulders: Moderate-Lighter the higher you go. No shoulders. Heavier on weekends.
Type/Difficulty: Steep mountain ride. Very Difficult.
Riding Time/Speed Assumption (Without Stops): 2 hours at 10 mph.
Start/End Point: Chautauqua Park at approximately Baseline Rd. & 9th St.
Best In Town/Path Ride to the Start: From the Creek Path, Chautauqua Route #1.
Directions: Ride west on Baseline which turns into Flagstaff Rd .at Gregory Canyon Park & to the picnic area on the left side of the road at the reservoir overlook. (9.5 m.)
Refueling Possibilities: None.
Additional Comments: Probably the most popular hill climb in the county. Above the turn off to the Amphitheater, the climb gets considerably steeper until you reach the downhill portion.
Skinny Tire Variations:

    S1. Amphitheater. The most common option is to turn right (north) at the Amphitheater turnoff and continue 1/2 mile to the parking lot/overlook. This becomes 8 miles up and back for a total of 1,200 feet from Chautauqua Park.

    S2. Super Flagstaff. Continue past the Amphitheater turn-off for another mile and a half until you pass the 5 mile marker and the road levels at the exit to the Mountain Park. This is 2,000 feet of climbing and just over 10 miles round trip.
Fat Tire Possibilities:

    F1. Walker Ranch-Meyers Gulch at mile 6.6 on the right (west) offers some fire road riding for 2.5 miles (one way) and 700 feet of elevation.

    F2. Walker Ranch-Boulder Creek at mile 6.8 on the left (south) a single track trail loops down through the Boulder Creek valley.

    F3. Crescent Junction. At the end of the main route, turn left at the reservoir picnic grounds/overlook onto a gravel road which goes below the dam and continues out to Coal Creek Canyon at Crescent Junction. (6.7 miles)

    F4. Magnolia Road. If you continue straight past the reservoir overlook toward the west at the end of the main route, the road splits. Take the right hand fork and the road soon turns to gravel. After about a mile the road turns into a 4WD/mountain bike only 2-track. The 4WD section lasts about a mile and then the road improves. Continue on this road for another 2.5 miles and you will dead end into Magnolia Road. If you turn right on Magnolia Rd. you will arrive at Boulder Canyon (Colo. 119) after about 7 miles. If you turn left on Magnolia Rd., after about 3 miles you will end up about a mile west of Pinecliffe on Colo. 72.

    F4a. Gross Reservoir 4WD. From the 4WD road to the west of the picnic grounds in the route above, look for 4WD trails on the left (south) that go back into Gross Reservoir. There are many possibilities.

Nelson Road Loop
23 miles & 1,000 feet of climbing

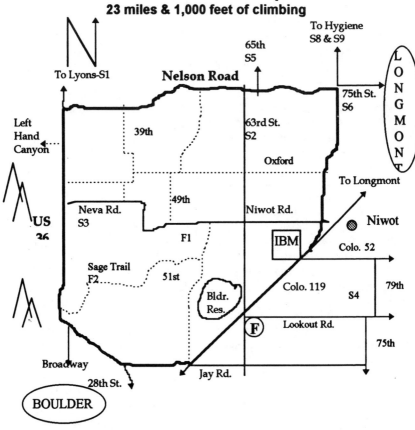

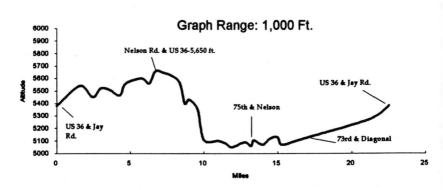

Graph Range: 1,000 Ft.

Main Route
13. NELSON ROAD/75TH LOOP

Mileage (loop): 23 Miles
Total Altitude Gain: 1,000 Feet
Steepness: The descent down Nelson Rd. averages between 2.5% and 3% for about 4 miles.
Traffic Volume/Existence of Shoulders: US 36 and Colo. 119 (Longmont Diagonal) have high traffic volume and good shoulders. Nelson Road and 75th have low traffic volume and no shoulders. Jay Road has shoulders and fairly high traffic volume.
Type/Difficulty: Rolling plains. Low difficulty if no wind.
Riding Time/Speed Assumption (Without Stops): 1 hour and 20 minutes at 17 mph.
Start/End Point: The corner of Jay Road and US 36 north of Boulder.
Best In Town/Path Ride to the Start: Wonderland Lake Route # 4 (Option S1) from the west side of town. About 1/2 mile before reaching US 36 turn right (east) on Yarmouth Rd. to US 36. Turn right on US 36 and go SE about 1/4 mile to the start of the route. From the east side of town use Boulder Reservoir (Route #5) to Jay Road.
Directions(Clockwise): Ride north on US 36 to Nelson Road. (7.2 m.)

⌐ *Turn right (east) on Nelson Road* to 75th St. (5.6 m.)

⌐ *Turn right (south) on 75th* (which takes a jog to the west and becomes 73rd St.) to Colo. 119 (4.6 m.)

⌐ *Turn right (southwest) on Colo. 119 (Longmont Diagonal)* to Jay Road. (3.9 m.)

⌐ *Turn right (west) on Jay Road* to US 36. (1.2 m.)

Refueling Possibilities: The only refreshments available on the route are at mile 1.4 at the go-cart/miniature golf/batting cages. If you wish to take side trips, at least two choices are available: Hygiene, just over 2 miles north of the corner of 75th and Nelson Road on 75th and, Gunbarrel, about 1/2 mile south on 63rd across the Diagonal Highway.
Additional Comments: The descent down Nelson Road has to be one of the best; long, fast and pedalable (if that is a word) in the county. A good training route due to few stop signs/lights. This is the route used by many of the triathlons run out of Boulder Reservoir. Watch for the birds of prey on Nelson Road.
Skinny Tire Variations:

S1. Lyons One possibility that is obvious and heavily biked but one which we recommend against is to continue north into Lyons on US 36. The problems are: the high traffic volume, the shoulder disappears just north of Nelson Road and the traffic is traveling at high speed. A better route into Lyons is to ride north through Hygiene on 75th then west on Colo. 66 to Lyons. See Main Route for Lyons #17.

S2. 63rd St. To shorten the route you can turn right (south) on 63rd from Nelson Rd. at mile 10 to the Diagonal, then continue on the main route. This takes about 5 miles off the main route as described above.

S3. Neva/Niwot Road Short Loop Clockwise Niwot Road can be worked into this route (mainly to shorten the ride) in many ways. Turn right(east) onto Neva Rd. from US 36 (Neva becomes Niwot Rd.) and continue to 63rd or 75th for a shorter loop.(US 36/Niwot Rd./63rd/Colo. 119 loop-13.6 miles, 450 feet in climbing)

S3a Colo. 119 Avoidance. To avoid returning on the Diagonal, take a right (west) on Niwot Road from 73rd at about mile 16 to 63rd, then left (south) on 63rd and cross the Diagonal Highway on 63rd and continue to Jay Road. Turn right (west) on Jay Road and continue straight across the Diagonal again to US 36.

S4. Return to the east end of the Boulder Creek Bike Path at Valmont and 55th, refer to the above variation and instead of turning onto Jay Road from 63rd, continue south until 63rd turns into 61st and dead ends into Valmont and turn right (west) to about 55th.

S5. St. Vrain Road To lengthen the ride by about 3 miles, from the corner of Nelson and 65th, turn left (north) on 65th to St. Vrain Rd.. Turn right (east) where 65th ends onto St. Vrain Rd.. Ride east to where St. Vrain Rd. dead ends into 75th, then turn right (south) back onto 75th and continue back to Nelson Road.

S6. Longmont-Heading further east of 75th on Nelson Rd. or Hygiene Rd. will quickly get you into western Longmont.

S7. 75th South of Colo. 119 to east end of Creek Path-Another possible return to east Boulder is to turn left (east) onto Colo. 52 shortly after joining Colo. 119. Ride east on Colo. 52 about 2 miles to 79th. Turn right (south) on 79th to its end at Lookout Rd. Turn right (west) on Lookout Rd. to 75th. (Another shorter but busier option is to use 71st to cross between 52 & Lookout. You must turn left (east) on Lookout to 75th.) Turn south on 75th to Valmont Rd. Turn right (west) on Valmont to about 55th where the entrance to the Creek path exits to the right (north).

S8. Carter Lake See Route #20 for longer possibilities to the north.

S9. Colo. 66 East See Route #19 for loops to the east along I-25 frontage road.

Fat Tire Possibilities:

F1. Boulder Reservoir to Rabbit Mountain Trails. There are a string of gravel roads leading north. From the corner of 51st and Jay Road ride north on 51st on the gravel to Niwot Rd. Turn left (west) on Niwot Rd. to 49th and turn right (north). 49th runs north from Niwot Rd. to Oxford and jogs east to 51st to Nelson Rd. Turn left (west) on Nelson Rd. to 51st. Turn right (north) on 51st to St. Vrain Rd. Turn right (east) on St. Vrain to 59th St.. Turn left (north) on 59th to Hygiene Rd. Turn right (east) on Hygiene Rd. to 61st. Turn left (north) on 61st which turns into 63rd out to Colo. 66. Turn left (west) on Colo. 66 to 61st. Turn right (north) on 61st to the Rabbit Mountain Trailhead. 24 miles round trip to trailhead. Currently there are about 6 miles of mostly double track, hilly mountain bike riding in the Rabbit Mountain Open Space but this could expand shortly.

F1a 38th/39th/41st between Nelson & Neva Rd-Another gravel road option between Nelson & Neva Rds is 38th/39th/41st about 1 mile east of US 36. To join with the F1 variation riding north, leave Neva Rd. just east of US 36 and ride north on 38th Follow 38th east to 39th and then east again to 41st. to Nelson Rd. Turn right (east) on Nelson Rd. to 51st. and turn left (north), joining the F1 route above at Nelson Rd.

F2. Boulder Res./Sage/Eagle Trail Loop-See In Town/Path Ride #5 for details.

Peak to Peak Hwy(Colo. 72) from Coal Creek to Colo. 7

26 miles one way and 2,000 feet of climbing

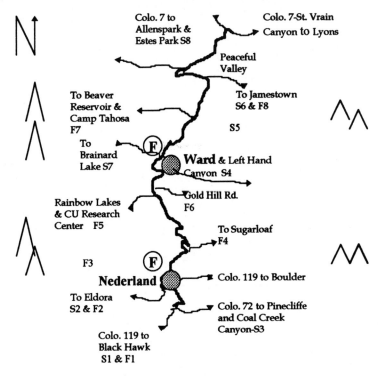

Colo. 7 to Allenspark & Estes Park S8

Colo. 7-St. Vrain Canyon to Lyons

Peaceful Valley

To Beaver Reservoir & Camp Tahosa F7

To Jamestown S6 & F8

S5

To Brainard Lake S7

F

Ward & Left Hand Canyon S4

Gold Hill Rd. F6

Rainbow Lakes & CU Research Center F5

To Sugarloaf F4

F3

F

Nederland

Colo. 119 to Boulder

To Eldora S2 & F2

Colo. 72 to Pinecliffe and Coal Creek Canyon-S3

Colo. 119 to Black Hawk S1 & F1

Graph Range: 3,000 Ft.

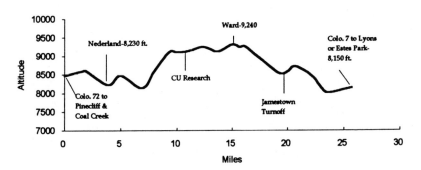

Main Route
14. Peak To Peak Hwy(Colo. 72)-Colo. 119 to Colo. 7

Mileage(one way): 26 Miles
Total Altitude Gain: 2,000 Feet
Steepness: Miles 7-9 (about 4 miles N. of Nederland) sustain an average grade of 7.7% climbing on the northbound trip. About 3 miles south of Colo. 7 the grade is about 7.5% for about a mile climbing on the southbound trip. The rest of the climbs are between 1 and 5%.
Traffic Volume/Existence of Shoulders: Medium traffic volume with wide shoulders except for the first 4 miles from Colo. 119 to Nederland.
Type/Difficulty: Rolling. Medium difficulty.
Riding Time/Speed Assumption (Without Stops): 1 hour 45 minutes at 15 mph.
Start/End Point: At the south end, go up Colo. 72 (Coal Creek Canyon) over Wondervu, through Pinecliffe to the intersection of Colo. 119 and Colo. 72. This is where this route starts. Some may decide to drive to this point or Nederland where the wider shoulder continues north. The north end is at the intersection of Colo. 72 and Colo. 7 at the top of St. Vrain Canyon just SE of Allenspark.

Best In Town/Path Ride to the Start: To start at the south end Marshall Route #6 to Pinecliffe Main Route #18. At the north end Wonderland Lake Route #4 (Option S1) from the west side of town or Boulder Reservoir Route #5 to Jay Rd. then west on Jay Rd. to US 36. Turn right (northwest) on US 36 to junction with Broadway. See Allenspark Main Route #23.

Directions: Ride north on Colo. 72.

↵ The only turn you must make is in Nederland (mile 3.9). Here you must *turn left in town to stay on Colo. 72.*

Refueling Possibilities: There is a restaurant at about mile 2. There are several stores and restaurants in Nederland. There is the general store in Ward (off Colo. 72 about 1/2 mile and down a fairly steep hill into town). Just north of the Ward turn off is a restaurant. At the north end you might continue into Allenspark or Raymond (see Allenspark route).

Additional Comments: For lack of traffic, wide shoulders, great scenery and a good rolling ride, this stretch of road cannot be beat in Boulder County.

Skinny Tire Variations: This route, or portions of it, can be worked into many scenarios. From south to north here are some suggestions:

S1. Rollinsville. From the south end of this route go south on Colo. 119 2 miles to Rollinsville. There is no shoulder for about 200 yards; then there is a wide shoulder to Rollinsville.

S2. Eldora. About 1 mile south of Nederland is the road leading west to the town of Eldora. 4 miles and 400 feet to the end of the pavement

S3. Coal Creek/St. Vrain Canyon Loop. (The Boulder Mountain Road Race) For a mega mountain ride, take a round trip from Boulder up Coal Creek Canyon, over this route, down St. Vrain to Lyons, then back to Boulder. (93 miles and 7,500 feet gain). This was a part of the Red Zinger/Coors Classic Bicycle Race. The record for the course is held by Mark Pringle in 3:56:50 in 1977 with an average speed of 23.56 mph.

S4. Ward. Same as above (S3) except turn right into Ward and descend through Left Hand Canyon and back to Boulder. (75 miles and 6500 feet gain).

S5. Left Hand Canyon/St. Vrain Canyon Loop. Leave Altona on US 36 between Boulder and Lyons and ride up Left Hand Canyon to Ward (Route #18), head north on Colo. 72 to Colo. 7 and descend down St. Vrain canyon to Lyons (Route #23). Continue east on Colo. 7 to 75th; turn south to Nelson road. Turn right (west) on Nelson Rd. to US36. Turn left on US 36 to Altona. We do not recommend US 36 from Nelson Rd to Lyons due to lack of shoulder and traffic volume. (56 miles and 4,800 ft gain).

S6 Jamestown. 5 miles north of Ward turn east. Only 2.5 miles of gravel over rolling terrain leads to a nice loop through Jamestown. See route #15 for details.

S7 Brainard Lake. About 100 yards north of the north Ward turnoff is the road to Brainard Lake to the west. 10 miles 1,100 feet up & back at an average grade of 4.2%.

S8 Allenspark and Estes Park. See Routes #23 & #25.

We prefer to avoid Boulder Canyon and we highly recommend others to do the same due to traffic volume, lack of shoulders and sharp curves. We, therefore, do not include that as a variation.

Fat Tire Possibilities: Again, the opportunities are many. From south to north they are:

F1. Rollins Pass/Winter Park. From Rollinsville (S1 above) turn west on the gravel road (16 Rd). Ride about 7 miles to the turn off to the right (north) to Moffat Rd. (FR 149) and ride it over Rollins Pass to Winter Park. Rollins to Winter Park 35 miles and about 4,000 feet of climbing one way. Call Roosevelt/Arapahoe National Forest Office in Boulder to assure the road is open (303-444-6600).

F2. 4th of July Campground. Follow variation S2 to the end of the pavement in Eldora then continue west for 8+ miles one way from Colo. 72.

F3. Caribou. About a mile west/north of Nederland on Colo. 72 is a gravel road (128 Rd.) leading to Caribou, about 5 miles one way.

F4. Sugarloaf. About 3 miles north of Nederland is 122 Rd., a gravel road leading to the east and the Town of Sugarloaf in about 6 miles. See 4-mile Canyon route #9 for more possibilities from Sugarloaf.

F5. Rainbow Lakes. 7.2 miles north of Nederland (4 miles south of Ward) is the gravel turn off to U. of Colo. Alpine Research Center and Rainbow Lakes Campground toward the west. The campground is about 5 miles from the highway.

F5a. Rainbow Lakes to Caribou. About a mile before the campground is a four wheel drive road off to the left (southeast) which will eventually lead to Caribou (see F3 above).

F6. Gold Hill. Just over 3 miles south of Ward is Gold Hill Rd. (52 Rd.), a gravel road leading east to the town of Gold Hill. 7 miles one way. See Sunshine Canyon-Gold Hill variation Route #9 Option F2 for details on returning to Boulder.

F7. Beaver Reservoir. About 3 miles north of Ward is a sign for Camp Tahosa and forest access. This is a gravel road which leads up to Beaver Reservoir and dead ends into an ashram. The Sourdough and South St. Vrain trails cross this road if you wish to venture on to some rugged trail riding. (3.4 miles to dead end)

F8. Jamestown. About 5 miles north of Ward is 94 Rd.-a gravel road for 2.4 miles then pavement for 4.3 miles to Jamestown. (Route #15).

Jamestown
27 miles up & back-1,700 feet of climbing

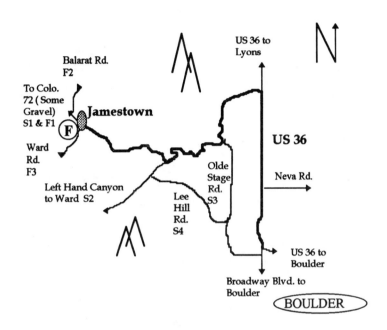

Graph Range: 2,000 Ft.

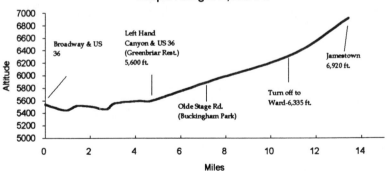

Main Route
15. JAMESTOWN

Mileage(up and back): 27 Miles
Total Altitude Gain: 1,700 Feet
Steepness: The average grade from US 36 to Jamestown is 3%. The steepest portion is above the Ward turnoff where the grade averages 4.5%.
Traffic Volume/Existence of Shoulders: High traffic on US 36 with wide shoulders. Low to Medium traffic volume; no shoulders in the canyon.
Type/Difficulty: Gradual climb up. Medium difficulty.
Riding Time/Speed Assumption (Without Stops): Up-1 hour 45 minutes at 9 mph. Down 30 minutes at about 20 mph.
Start/End Point: North end of Broadway where it merges with US 36.

Best In Town/Path Ride to the Start: Wonderland Lake Route #4 (Option S1) from the west side of town or Boulder Reservoir Route #5 to Jay Rd. then west on Jay Rd. to US 36. Turn right (northwest) on US 36 to junction with Broadway.
Directions: Ride north on US 36 to Altona at the corner of US 36 and Left Hand Canyon (Greenbrier Restaurant). (4.7 m.)

    ⌐ *Turn left at Left Hand Canyon.* (6.2 m.)

    ⌐ *Bear right at the split to Jamestown* or Ward. (2.5 m.)

Refueling Possibilities: The store in Jamestown is usually well stocked.
Additional Comments: A very steady climb. The road becomes much steeper beyond the town and turns to gravel about 4 miles beyond Jamestown. The gravel stretch is only about 2 1/2 miles long and not too steep so you can continue out to Peak to Peak (Colo. 72) without a mountain bike.
Skinny Tire Variations:

    S1. Peak to Peak Hwy. Continue through Jamestown 4.3 miles to the end of the pavement (from Balarat Rd. to the top of the steep portion-a distance of 2.5 miles-the grade averages 8.3%) or another 2.4 miles beyond the end of the pavement to Peak to Peak Hwy. (See Route #14)

    S2. Ward. Split left at the Ward turn in Left Hand Canyon (see Left Hand Canyon/Ward Route #18)

    S3. Olde Stage Road. To add a significant hill, the route may be started or returned from just south of the intersection of US 36 and Broadway at Lee Hill road and Broadway and travel over Olde Stage Road. To start the ride this way, turn west off of Broadway at Lee Hill Rd. Lee Hill Rd crosses Broadway about 1/2 mile south of where Broadway ends at US 36. Continue straight over Olde Stage Road at the intersection to Lee Hill. This meets Left Hand Canyon at Buckingham Park picnic grounds. To continue to Jamestown turn left when Olde Stage dead ends into Left Hand Canyon. To return via this route, turn right on to Olde Stage Road at the large picnic grounds off to the left. This adds about 400 feet of climbing and takes about 3 miles off of the main route.

    S4. Lee Hill Road is also a possible route for about 650 additional feet one way. Follow the above variation to the corner of Lee Hill Road and turn left onto Lee Hill (the first mile averages an 11% grade) and follow it through the mountain subdivision until it ends into Left Hand Canyon. Turn right at the dead end to rejoin the main route after a descent of about a mile.

Fat Tire Possibilities:

F1. Peak to Peak Hwy. Continue west to Peak to Peak highway near Peaceful Valley on pavement for 4.3 miles then 2.4 miles of wide 2 wheel drive gravel road. (6.7 miles Jamestown to Colo. 72).

F2. Balarat Rd. About a mile past (NW) of Jamestown is Balarat Rd. to the right (NE). This gravel 2WD road climbs about 700 ft and then descends 1,000 feet to St. Vrain Canyon at mile marker 24 on Colo. 7, for a total of about 7 miles one way.

F3. Ward via Ward Rd. About 50 yds west of the Post Office in Jamestown is Ward Rd. It is gravel and quickly turns into 4WD. It climbs SW about 3 miles to a ridge at 8,550 ft. To the right (west) about 1 mile is Gold Lake Ranch. This area has many 4WD roads leading in many directions. There are few landmarks and no signs. We have turned down many dead ends. Leave time to explore and get lost.

F3a. Loop back to Jamestown. From the top of the ridge at 8,550 ft turn left (east) and wander the myriad of 4WD trails. At least one of them leads back to Jamestown. Good Luck (see comments in F3).

Erie Loop
24 miles and 600 feet of climbing

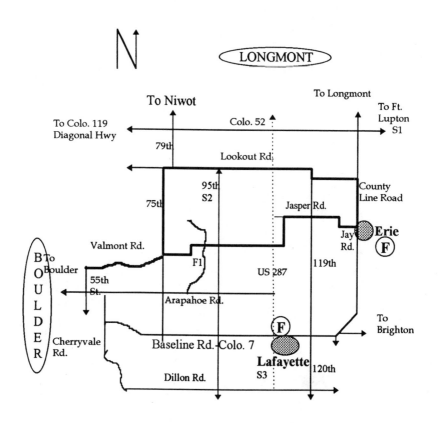

Graph Range: 1,500 ft.

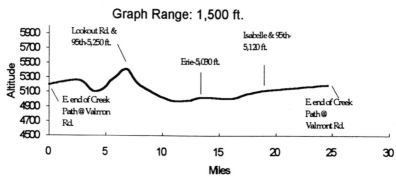

Main Route
16. ERIE LOOP

Mileage(loop): 24 Miles
Total Altitude Gain: 600 Feet
Traffic Volume/Existence of Shoulders: Low to Moderate. Little or no shoulders.
Type/Difficulty: Rolling plains. Low difficulty except for 1 long, gradual hill.
Riding Time/Speed Assumption (Without Stops): 1 hour 40 minutes at 15 mph.
Start/End Point: East end of the Boulder Creek Path at Valmont.
Best In Town/Path Ride to the Start: Boulder Creek Path Route #7-east end.
Directions: Ride east on Valmont to 75th (2.6 m.).

⌐ *Turn left (north) on 75th* to Lookout Road (2.8 m.).

⌐ *Turn right (east) on Lookout Road* to its end at 115th St. (5.1 m.).

⌐ *Turn right (south) on 115th St.* curve east on to Kenosha to its end at County Line Road (1.7 m.).

⌐ *Turn right (south) on County Line Road;* ride to Erie and the intersection with Jay Rd. (1.3 m.).

⌐ *Turn right (west) on Jay Rd.* through the jog to the north where Jay Rd. becomes Jasper Rd. and on to 109th St. (2.5 m.).

⌐ *Turn left (south) on 109th St.* to Isabelle Rd. (1.5 m.).

⌐ *Turn right (west) on Isabelle Rd.* to its end at 95th St. (1.5 m.).

⌐ *Turn right (north) on 95th St. to Valmont Rd.* (.2 m.).

⌐ *Turn left (west) at Valmont Rd.* to the starting point. (5.3 mile)

Refueling Possibilities: Erie has several restaurants, grocery stores and gas stations.
Additional Comments: A mostly quiet and relatively flat ride.
Skinny Tire Variations:

S1. Ft. Lupton & Beyond. Jog north on County Line Rd. to Colo. 52 turn right (east) and continue east on Colo. 52 to Ft. Lupton and beyond. See Ft. Lupton Main Route #19.

S2. 95th St. Loop. Turn right (south) on 95th to Valmont Rd. Turn right (west) on Valmont and return to the end of the Creek Path. (16 mile round trip).

S3. Continue South to Dillon Rd. Another return to Boulder (less traffic) is to turn left (south) on 119th St. to the east side of Lafayette. Cross Colo. 7 (Baseline Rd.) and the road jogs east to 120th St.. Follow 120th to its end at Dillon Rd. Turn right (west) on Dillon Rd. to US 36. Cross US 36 and turn right (north) on Marshall Rd. Ride NW on Marshall Rd. to Cherryvale. Turn right (north) on Cherryvale to its end at Arapahoe Rd. . Cross Arapahoe and turn left (west) on the bike path. Ride across the creek and turn right (north) onto S. Boulder Creek Greenway Trail. Follow this north to the junction with Boulder Creek Path. This adds about 10 miles to the main route.

Fat Tire Possibilities:

     F1. <u>Teller Farms/White Rocks Trail</u>. 4.5 miles east of the intersection of the Boulder Creek path and Valmont Rd. are some great fat tire trails. From Valmont Rd. between 75th & 95th St.(closer to 95th) at the East Boulder Trailhead parking lot ride south on Teller Farm trail. The trail ends at a parking lot off of Arapahoe Rd. after a flat ride of 2.2 miles.

To the north is White Rocks trail. From the parking lot ride west about 100 yards, cross Valmont and ride north on the trail. This trail climbs to Gunbarrel Farm trail and continues to climb to a water tower and then descends to the trail head at the intersection of Boulderado & Cambridge Streets in Gunbarrel, about 4 miles one way. The total trip from the end of the Creek path, to the end of both trails and back is about 21 miles and 850 feet of climbing.

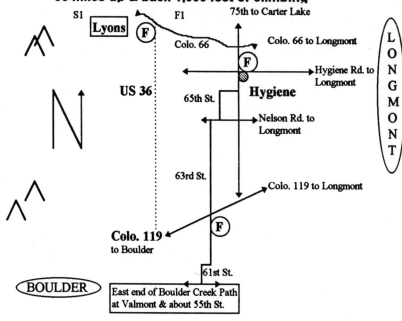

Lyons (Avoiding US 36)
38 miles up & back-1,000 feet of climbing

S1   Lyons   (F)   F1   75th to Carter Lake

Colo. 66   Colo. 66 to Longmont

(F)   Hygiene Rd. to Longmont

US 36   65th St.   Hygiene

Nelson Rd. to Longmont

63rd St.   Colo. 119 to Longmont

Colo. 119   (F)
to Boulder

61st St.

BOULDER   East end of Boulder Creek Path
at Valmont & about 55th St.

LONGMONT

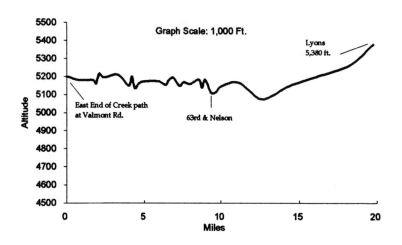

Graph Scale: 1,000 Ft.

Lyons
5,380 ft.

East End of Creek path
at Valmont Rd.

63rd & Nelson

Altitude — Miles

Main Route
17. LYONS avoiding US 36

Special Note: Due to the lack of shoulders and heavy traffic north of Nelson Rd. on US 36 we suggest using 75th St. through Hygiene. As of this printing, US 36 is scheduled to be widened in 1997. After widening, US 36 should be safer.

Mileage(up and back): 38 Miles

Total Altitude Gain: 1,000 Feet

Traffic Volume/Existence of Shoulders: Low to moderate traffic and few shoulders.

Type/Difficulty: Rolling plains. Medium difficulty.

Riding Time/Speed Assumption (Without Stops): Just over 3 hours at 12 mph.

Start/End Point: East end of Boulder Creek Bike Path at about 55th and Valmont Road.

Best In Town/Path Ride to the Start: Boulder Creek Path Route #7-east end.

Directions: Ride east on Valmont to 61st. (.8 m.)

⌐ *Turn left (north) on 61st,* which jogs over to become 63rd, until it dead ends into Nelson Road. (8.6 m.)

⌐ *Turn right (east) on Nelson Road* to 65th. (.3 m)

⌐ *Turn left (north) on 65th* which dead ends into St. Vrain. (1.5 m.)

⌐ *Turn right (east) on St. Vrain Road* to 75th. (1.3 m.)

⌐ *Turn left (north) on 75th* through Hygiene to Colo. 66. (1.9 m.)

⌐ *Turn left (west) on Colo. 66* and continue to Lyons. (5 m.)

Refueling Possibilities: Colo. 119 & 63rd, Hygiene and Lyons.

Additional Comments: This route, with the Apple Valley variation, is another classic ride. Riders (often Boulder's best) would meet at the topless bar called the Bustop on Tues. & Thurs. evenings and ride this route. Many times, hundreds of riders would pedal north in a pack. Police busts became an annual affair since the riders frequently failed to follow the single file law and sometimes ignored stop signs. These busts occasionally sported helicopters and headline news.

Skinny Tire Variations:

S1. Apple Valley (The venerable Bustop Route-see above) At the corner of Colo. 7 and US 36 at the west end of Lyons split right on US 36 and ride about .3 mile to Apple Valley Rd. on the left. Follow Apple Valley Rd. out to US 36 and return on US 36 to Lyons where you rejoin the main route. Adds about 6 miles and 120 feet to the main route.

Fat Tire Options:

F1. Rabbit Mountain-See Rabbit Mtn Fat Tire Option for Nelson Rd. Loop Main Route #13 Option F1.

Ward via Left Hand Canyon
46 miles up and back-4,100 feet of climbing

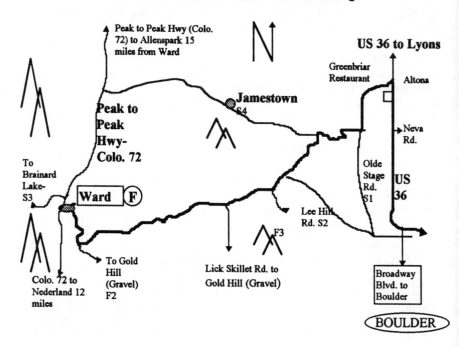

Peak to Peak Hwy (Colo. 72) to Allenspark 15 miles from Ward

N

US 36 to Lyons

Greenbriar Restaurant

Altona

Jamestown
S4

Peak to Peak Hwy-Colo. 72

Neva Rd.

To Brainard Lake-S3

Olde Stage Rd. S1

US 36

Ward F

Lee Hill Rd. S2

To Gold Hill (Gravel) F2

F3

Colo. 72 to Nederland 12 miles

Lick Skillet Rd. to Gold Hill (Gravel)

Broadway Blvd. to Boulder

BOULDER

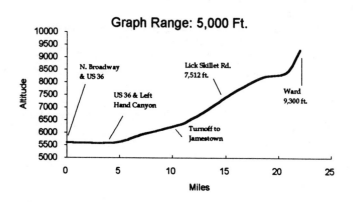

Graph Range: 5,000 Ft.

N. Broadway & US 36

Lick Skillet Rd. 7,512 ft.

US 36 & Left Hand Canyon

Ward 9,300 ft.

Turnoff to Jamestown

Altitude

Miles

Main Route
18. WARD via LEFT HAND CANYON

Mileage(up and back): 46 Miles
Total Altitude Gain: 4,100 Feet
Steepness: This one is deceiving. The average grade from US 36 to Ward is only 4% for 18 miles. It starts slowly at about 2.2% for 6 miles to the Jamestown turnoff. The next 4 miles average 4% to 4.5%, followed by 3 miles of 5.4%. Next is a short respite of 2% then it finishes with a whopping mile and a half of 10% grade.
Traffic Volume/Existence of Shoulders: High traffic on US 36 with wide shoulders. Low to Medium traffic volume, no shoulders in the canyon.
Type/Difficulty: Long gradual climb up. Very difficult.
Riding Time/Speed Assumption (Without Stops): Up-3 hours at 8 mph. Down-1 hour at about 23 mph.
Start/End Point: North end of Broadway where it merges with US 36.
Best In Town/Path Ride to the Start: Wonderland Lake Route #4 (Option S1) from the west side of town or Boulder Reservoir Route #5 to Jay Rd. then west on Jay Rd. to US 36. Turn right (northwest) on US 36 to junction with Broadway.
Directions: Ride north on US 36 to Altona at the corner of US 36 and Left Hand Canyon (Greenbrier Restaurant). (4.7 m.)
    ↵ *Turn left (west) Left Hand Canyon* turn off. (6.2 m.)
    ↵ *Turn left (south) to Ward at the split between Ward and Jamestown*. (11.3 m.)
Refueling Possibilities: The store in Ward on the route has drinks and snacks.
Additional Comments: A very steady climb which gets generally steeper the higher you ride.
Skinny Tire Variations:
    S1. Olde Stage Road. To add a significant hill (400 feet in additional altitude one way) you may start or return from just south of the intersection of US 36 and Broadway at Lee Hill road and Broadway and travel over Olde Stage Road. To start the ride this way, turn west off of Broadway at Lee Hill Road. Lee Hill Road crosses Broadway about 1/2 mile south of where Broadway ends at US 36. Continue straight over Olde Stage Road at the intersection with Lee Hill Rd. This meets Left Hand Canyon at Buckingham Park picnic grounds. To continue to Ward turn left when Olde Stage dead ends into Left Hand Canyon. To return via this route, turn right on to Olde Stage Road at the large picnic grounds off to the left.
    S2. Lee Hill Road is also a possible route for about 450 additional feet one way. Follow the above variation to the corner of Lee Hill Road and turn left onto Lee Hill (the first mile averages an 11% grade) and follow it through the mountain subdivision until it ends into Left Hand Canyon.
    S3. Brainard Lake. To add 10 miles up & back with about 1,100 additional feet in altitude at about an average 4.2% grade continue straight through Ward to Colo. 72 turn right (north) on 72 for about 100 yards & turn left (west) toward Brainard Lake.
    S4. Jamestown. Loop over to Jamestown by heading north from Ward on Hwy 72 for 5 miles to 94 Rd. Turn right on gravel for 2.5 miles then pavement for 4 more miles into Jamestown and finally 2.5 miles back into Lefthand Canyon. This route adds about 3.5 miles to the main route

Fat Tire Possibilities:

   F1. Lick Skillet Rd. to Gold Hill. 11 miles up the canyon from US 36 is Lick Skillet Rd. (gravel) up and to the left (south). A one mile & 800 ft steep gravel road climbs into Gold Hill-a grueling 15% grade!.

   F2. Gold Hill-5.5 miles west of Lick Skillet Rd. is 95 Rd., a gravel road leading back up to the left (SE). After about a mile the road ends at Gold Hill Rd. (52 Rd.) Turn left (east) to Gold Hill after about 6 miles. 7 miles from Left Hand Canyon to Gold Hill.

   F3. Rowena to Sunshine. About 2.5 miles west of Lee Hill & Lefthand is a group of homes near the road. This is Rowena. A 4WD road ascends southeast from the road and climbs to Sunshine Saddle. From there a road can be found heading south. It goes through Sunshine townsite and continues out to Sunshine Canyon road at the end of the pavement. See route #9 for more details.

Please see the Peak to Peak route #14 and Jamestown route #15 for other variations.

Fort Lupton-East of I-25
52 miles out & back and 1,400 ft. of Climbing

GREELEY

N

To Greeley
S6

Colo. 60

Johnstown
S5

Berthoud

Colo. 56

19
Rd.

Lyons

US
287

Colo. 66

I-25/
Frontage
Rd.

Platteville

Hygiene

75th

Longmont

US
85

Colo.
119

Rd.
7
S1

13
Rd.
S4

Colo. 52

Firestone

Lookout Rd.

Dacono

F

Jay Rd.

75th

Ft. Lupton

E. end
Creek Path

Valmont Rd.

Baseline Rd. Colo. 7

S2

US
36

Dillon Rd.

Washington St. to
Northglenn/Denver
S3

NORTHGLENN

Graph Range: 1,500 Ft.

79th &
Lookout Rd.
5,325 ft.

County Line
& Colo. 52

Ft. Lupton
4,800 ft.

Altitude

E. end of Creek
Path @ Valmont
Rd.

| 5900 |
| 5700 |
| 5500 |
| 5300 |
| 5100 |
| 4900 |
| 4700 |
| 4500 |

0   5   10   15   20   25   30

Miles

Main Route
19. Fort Lupton/I-25 Frontage Rd. & East Options
Including Denver & Greeley

Mileage(out & back): 52 miles
Total Altitude Gain: 1,400 feet
Traffic Volume/Existence of Shoulders: Occasional heavy traffic on Colo. 52 but wide shoulders.
Type/Difficulty: Plains ride with some hills. Moderate difficulty.
Riding Time/Speed Assumption(Without Stops): 4 hours at 13 mph.
Start/End Point: East end of Boulder Creek Path at Valmont Rd. about 55th St.
Best In Town/Path Ride to the Start: Boulder Creek Path Route # 7-east end.
Directions: : Ride east on Valmont to 75th (2.6 m.).

⌐ *Turn left (north) on 75th* to Lookout Road (2.8 m.).

⌐ *Turn right (east) on Lookout Road* to 79th St. (.6 m.).

⌐ *Turn left (north) on 79th St.* to Colo. 52 (1 m.).

⌐ *Turn right (east) on Colo. 52* up the big hill and continue east to Fort Lupton (18 miles).

Refueling Possibilities: Dacono, and mini-marts in Ft. Lupton are right on Colo. 52 just inside town limits.
Additional Comments: To be avoided in windy weather.
Skinny Tire Variations:

S1. Barbour Ponds State Recreation Area/Colo. 66 Loop-Turn left (north) on Weld Cnty Rd. 7 one mile west of I-25. Ride 5 miles north to Barbour Ponds. Turn right (east) at the end of the road. After one mile, go under I-25 and turn left (north) on the frontage road and ride 2.5 miles to Colo. 66. Turn left (west) on Colo. 66 for 11 miles to 75th. Turn left (south) on 75th through Hygiene to Nelson Road. Turn right (west) to 63rd. Turn left (south) on 63rd St. and follow back to Valmont. Turning right (west) on Valmont will bring you back to the start. About 48 mile loop.

S2. I-25 Frontage Rd.-A fairly quiet frontage road follows I-25 making it possible to ride north or south to another East/West road such as the variation above. The best East/West roads are:
- Baseline Rd. (Colo. 7) through Lafayette. If continuing east, a less traveled option is to stay to the left just east of I-25 and continue straight on Baseline Rd. instead of curving south to stay on Colo. 7 toward Brighton. This road continues out to I-76.
- Dillon Rd. through S. Louisville (144th Ave. farther east). Turn north on Washington to Baseline Rd. 3 miles. (30 mile loop)
- Colo. 52-6 miles north of Baseline Rd.(36 mile loop)
- Colo. 66 through north Longmont to 75th (see S1 above). 14 miles north of Baseline Rd.(52 mile loop)
- Colo. 56 through Berthoud to Carter Lake. 21 miles north of Baseline Rd.(66 mile loop)
It is about 12 miles straight east to I-25 from about 55th St,. so depending on how far north or south you ride, you can add the miles on Frontage Road to get your estimated total. The elevation gain will not vary massively from the main route unless you venture quite far north or south.

S3. Denver/South Platte River system From the corner of Dillon Rd. & Washington St.(see S2-Dillon Rd. above) turn right (south) on Washington St. to 136th St.. Turn left (east) on 136th to Colorado Blvd. Turn right (south) on Colorado Blvd.. You have the choice of riding on the road or the bike path on the west side of the road. At 120th the bike path changes to the east side of Colorado Blvd. At 110th the bike path leaves Colorado Blvd. toward the southeast and ends at Riverdale Blvd. Turn right (SW) on Riverdale Blvd., which has a bike lane/shoulder, and follow it to the intersection of 88th Ave. and look for the South Platte River bike path to the southwest. This paved path cuts SW across the Denver metro area about 25 miles one way, following the South Platte River as far as Chatfield Reservoir. (This connection with the trail is about 25 miles from Boulder).

Side trails will go to: Golden along the Clear Creek Trail, Cherry Creek Reservoir along Cherry Creek Trail, and Parker along the Centennial Trail to the Cherry Creek Greenway Trail. There are many side routes and more being added all the time. Call the Colorado State Parks at 303-866-3437 for the Denver Metro area map of bicycle trails if you wish to see a complete layout of this trail system.

S4. 13 Rd.-Colo. 66-19 Rd. Loop North from Dacono-On Colo. 52 two miles east of I-25 is Dacono. Turn north on 13 Rd. and go through Frederick & Firestone. Jog west on 18 Rd. back to 13 Rd. Continue north to Colo. 66 (8 miles north of Colo. 52). Turn right (east) on Colo. 66 three miles to 19 Rd. Turn right (south) on 19 Rd. back to Colo. 52. 22 mile loop-almost flat.(60 miles round-trip from Boulder)

S5. Colo. 60 Loop North from Dacono through Johnstown -Follow S4 above but continue north on 13 Rd. to Colo. 60. The return route has a slight variation around the St. Vrain Nuclear Power Plant. Bear to the left (east) on 38 Rd. where 19 Rd. dead ends. This will pass the power plant and dead end into 34 Rd. Turn right (west) and go 1/2 mile to 19 Rd. Turn left (south) and continue to Colo. 52. This adds 19 miles for a total loop of 43 miles out of Dacono. (81 miles round-trip from Boulder).

S6. Greeley-Follow S5 above. From Johnstown, ride east (2 miles) to 21 Rd. (Colo. 257). Turn left (north) on 21 Rd. and go three miles to 54 Rd. Turn right (east) on 54 Rd. and ride 9 miles to the SW corner of Greeley. (109 miles round-trip from Boulder).

Carter Lake
60 miles up & back-2,300 feet of climbing

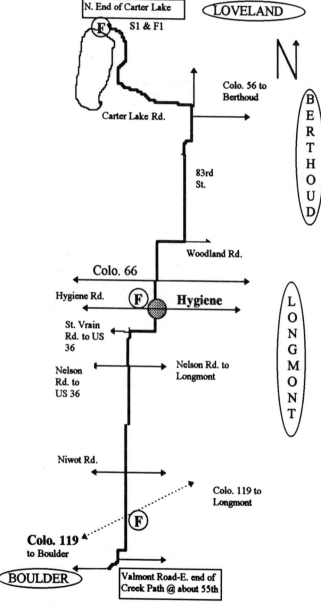

N. End of Carter Lake
S1 & F1
LOVELAND

Carter Lake Rd.

Colo. 56 to
Berthoud

N

BERTHOUD

83rd
St.

Woodland Rd.

Colo. 66

Hygiene Rd.   F   Hygiene

St. Vrain
Rd. to US
36

Nelson Rd. to
Longmont

Nelson
Rd. to
US 36

LONGMONT

Niwot Rd.

Colo. 119 to
Longmont

Colo. 119
to Boulder

F

BOULDER

Valmont Road-E. end of
Creek Path @ about 55th

Please see Altitude Graph on page 61.

Main Route
20. CARTER LAKE

Mileage(out and back): 60 Miles
Total Altitude Gain: 2,300 Feet
Steepness: The climb from the Ranger booth to the lake has an average grade of 6.4%.
Traffic Volume/Existence of Shoulders: Low to Moderate. No Shoulders. The road around the lake can be busy in the summer.
Type/Difficulty: Mostly flat until the rise to the lake. Low to medium difficulty
Riding Time/Speed Assumption(Without Stops): 4 hours at 15 mph.
Start/End Point: East end of Boulder Creek Bike path at the corner of 55th and Valmont Road.

Best In Town/Path Ride to the Start: Boulder Creek Path Route # 7-east end.
Directions: Ride east on Valmont to 61st. (.8 m.)

⌐ *Turn left (north) on 61st,* which jogs over to become 63rd, until it dead ends into Nelson Road. (8.6 m.)

⌐ *Turn right (east) on Nelson Road* to 65th. (.3 m)

⌐ *Turn left (north) on 65th* which dead ends into St. Vrain. (1.5 m.)

⌐ *Turn right (east) on St. Vrain Road* to 75th. (1.3 m.)

⌐ *Turn left (north) on 75th* through Hygiene & around the curve to the right (east) to 83rd (first major paved road heading north after the curve).(4.9 m.)

⌐ *Turn left (north) on 83rd* to its end into Colo. 56. (5.5 m.)
You will find yourself at the curve where Colo. 56 veers north.

⌐ *Turn left (west) on Colo. 56* and the road will quickly point you northward to the signs pointing out the road to Carter Lake. (.5 m.)

⌐ *Turn left (west) on the road to Carter Lake* to the split between the north and south ends of the lake. (3.6 m.)

⌐ *Turn right (west) toward the north end of the lake at the split* and continue to the shops at the north end of the lake. (3.4 m.)
Refueling Possibilities: Gunbarrel shopping center near the corner of the Diagonal and 63rd (mile 4). Hygiene at mile 13.4 has stores and restaurants. The north end of the lake has a small store and restaurant at the end of the route.
Additional Comments: The best time for this route is the Fall or Spring when the traffic around the lake is not as heavy. Watch for the cattle guards on the downhill return trip! This route is a favorite of many racers in the area.
Skinny Tire Variations:

S1. Pole Hill Road. Continue north at the end of the route and down to the road's end at Pole Hill road (1.5 m.). Turn right (east) on Pole Hill Road to the end of the road (2 m.). Turn left (north) on 29 Rd. .3 mile to 20th St.. Turn right (east) on 20th past Boedecker Lake to Namaqua/21st St. Turn right (south) on 21st and go 2 miles to 14th Rd.. Turn right (west) on 14th .8 mile to 23rd. Turn left (south) and it is 2.5 miles back to the Carter Lake turnoff.(if you don't mind a little gravel and want to shave some miles see Fat Tire route below for a variation on this route).

S1a. Masonville. Another possibility to add about 23 rural miles and about 200 feet out and back from Carter Lake is to continue north to Masonville. As above (S1), descend to Pole Hill Rd. and turn right. Ride east to 29 Rd. and turn left and continue north to US 34. Turn right (east) onto US 34 as if going in to Loveland but turn left (north) after .8 mile at Masonville Road. Big Thompson School is on the corner. Continue north 5.2 miles to the corner in Masonville. There is a store with refreshments there.

S1b. Estes Park. If you turn left on US 34, you are heading towards Estes Park up the Big Thompson Canyon. See Route #25.

Fat Tire Possibilities:

F1. Short Pole Hill Loop. From variation S1 turn right (south) on 29 Rd. (instead of left out to 20 Rd.) on to the gravel road at the east end of Pole Hill Road. This will lead you back to 23 Rd.-the north/south road to a point 1.5 miles north of Carter Lake Road.

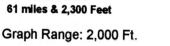

Carter Lake
61 miles & 2,300 Feet

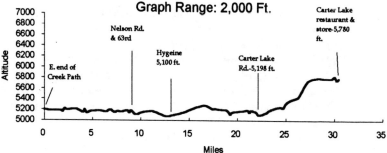

Pinecliffe via Coal Creek Canyon
63 mile out & back-5,740 feet of climbing

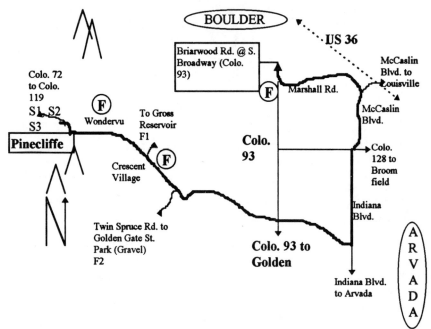

BOULDER

US 36

McCaslin Blvd. to Louisville

Briarwood Rd. @ S. Broadway (Colo. 93)

Marshall Rd.

McCaslin Blvd.

Colo. 72 to Colo. 119

S1 S2 S3

Wondervu

To Gross Reservoir F1

Pinecliffe

Crescent Village

Colo. 93

Colo. 128 to Broomfield

Indiana Blvd.

Twin Spruce Rd. to Golden Gate St. Park (Gravel) F2

Colo. 93 to Golden

Indiana Blvd. to Arvada

ARVADA

Graph Range: 5,000 Ft.

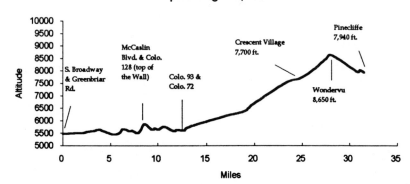

Pinecliffe 7,940 ft.

Crescent Village 7,700 ft.

McCaslin Blvd. & Colo. 128 (top of the Wall)

S. Broadway & Greenbriar Rd.

Colo. 93 & Colo. 72

Wondervu 8,650 ft.

Altitude

Miles

Main Route
21. COAL CREEK CANYON TO PINECLIFFE

Mileage(out and back): 63 Miles
Total Altitude Gain: 5,740 Feet
Steepness: An average grade of 4.7% is sustained from the start of the climb under the railroad tracks at the base of Coal Creek Canyon to Wondervu, about 9 miles. The steepness varies from about 2% to about 6.2% along the way. The descent from Wondervu to the west is also about 4.7% average drop.
Traffic Volume/Existence of Shoulders: The first part of the route has moderate traffic and a few stretches have shoulders. The canyon has no shoulders and fairly heavy traffic.
Type/Difficulty: Mountain ride. Long, steep climb. Difficult.
Riding Time/Speed Assumption (Without Stops): 4 hours at 15 mph.
Start/End Point: The south end of Broadway at the corner of Greenbriar and Broadway.
Best In Town/Path Ride to the Start: Marshall Route #6.
Directions: While the most direct route to Coal Creek Canyon from Boulder is to travel straight south on Colo. 93, we highly recommend against riding on Colo. 93 between Colo. 128 and Colo. 72. The traffic is very heavy, there are no shoulders and the traffic is traveling at very high speeds. Consequently, we recommend staying east on the Morgul-Bismark route to start; then over to Indiana Boulevard (not the safest road in the county but better than Colo. 93) on the east side of Rocky Flats until you reach Colo. 72, then head west and up the canyon. To get specific:

Ride south to Marshall/Colo. 170 on the bike path/side road or Colo. 93. (1.2 m.)

↵ *Turn left (east) on Marshall Road (Colo. 170).* If you are on 93, there is a stop light at Colo. 170. If you take the path/side road bear right at the intersection in the group of houses, then left to the intersection with Marshall Road (Colo. 170). In either case, ride east on 170 and curve south at US 36 to the road end intersection with McCaslin Boulevard. (3.8 m.)

↵ *Turn right (south) at the stop sign onto McCaslin Boulevard* to the road end at Colo. 128. (3.5 m.)

↵ *Turn left (east) onto Colo. 128* to Indiana Boulevard. (.3 m.)

↵ *Turn right (south) onto Indiana Boulevard* past the east entrance of Rocky Flats to stop sign at Colo. 72. (4.2 m.)

↵ *Turn right (west) on Colo. 72* to Pinecliffe. (18.5 m.)

Refueling Possibilities: At mile 24.7, well up into the canyon, there is a gas/food store. Wondervu (mile 28.1) also offers year-round restaurants and an ice cream shop in the Summer. Pinecliffe also offers restaurant and grocery shops.
Additional Comments: Outside of Boulder canyon, this is probably the busiest canyon in the county. The traffic lessens the higher you ride. Maybe the best way to ride this is to drive up to the corner of Colo. 72 and Colo. 93 and bike up from there.

Skinny Tire Variations:

S1. Peak to Peak Hwy. Continue west to Peak to Peak highway from Pinecliffe and descend Left Hand canyon or St. Vrain canyon. See Peak to Peak Highway route #14, Ward route #18 or Allenspark route #23 for details.(3.5 miles from Pinecliffe to Colo. 119 intersection)

S2. Rollinsville-From the intersection of Colo. 72 (exiting Coal Creek Canyon to the west) & Colo. 119 (see S1 above) turn south on Colo. 119 two miles to Rollinsville.

S3. Golden Gate State Park-Ride south on Colo. 119 from Rollinsville (see S2 above) for 5 miles to Golden Gate Canyon Rd. (Colo. 46). Turn left (east) 5 miles to Park Visitor Center. See Golden Gate route #22 for details of making this a loop of 85 miles.

Fat Tire Possibilities:

F1. Gross Reservoir. Turn right in Crescent Junction to Gross Reservoir. (see Gross Reservoir route #12 for details).

F2. Golden Gate State Park. Turn left on Twin Spruce/Gap Road (7 miles up Coal Creek Canyon from Colo. 93). Climb on pavement for two miles then the road turns to gravel. Three miles past the end of the pavement, you will enter Golden Gate State Park. After another 3.5 miles Mountain Base Rd. turns off to the left (south). This leads 3.2 miles south to Golden Gate Canyon Rd. about 1.2 miles west of the Visitor's Center. If you continue west on Gap Road for 1.2 more miles, it will bring you out to Colo. 119. (10 miles from Coal Creek to Colo. 119)

Golden Gate State Park
70 miles out & back-6,000 feet in climbing

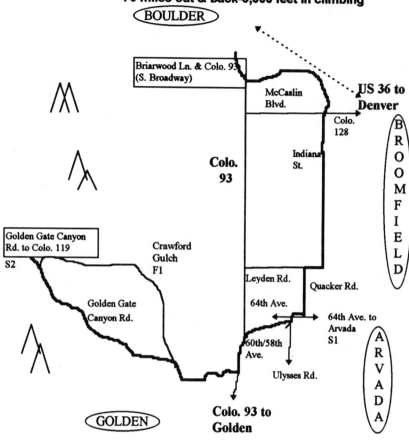

BOULDER

Briarwood Ln. & Colo. 93
(S. Broadway)

McCaslin Blvd.

US 36 to Denver

Colo. 128

Indiana St.

Colo. 93

BROOMFIELD

Golden Gate Canyon Rd. to Colo. 119
S2

Crawford Gulch F1

Golden Gate Canyon Rd.

Leyden Rd.

Quacker Rd.

64th Ave.

64th Ave. to Arvada
S1

60th/58th Ave.

Ulysses Rd.

ARVADA

GOLDEN

Colo. 93 to Golden

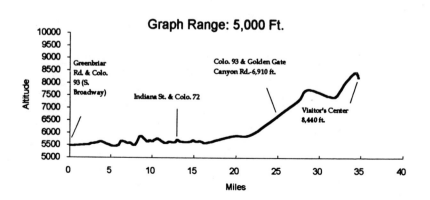

Graph Range: 5,000 Ft.

Altitude

Greenbriar Rd. & Colo. 93 (S. Broadway)

Indiana St. & Colo. 72

Colo. 93 & Golden Gate Canyon Rd.-6,910 ft.

Visitor's Center 8,440 ft.

Miles

Main Route
22. GOLDEN GATE PARK/WEST DENVER

Special note: Although this can be a beautiful ride, heavy traffic on Colo. 93 and in Golden Gate Canyon,(plus Colo. 119 and Colo. 72, if doing the loop) can completely spoil this route. It is best to ride this during the week or very early on weekends.

Mileage(out and back): 70 miles.

Total Altitude Gain: 6,000 feet.

Steepness: The average grade from Colo. 93 to the Park Visitor's Center is about 6.5% with the steeper section near the top at over 10% grade for about a mile.

Traffic Volume/Existence of Shoulders: Moderate to low traffic. Few shoulders.

Type/Difficulty: Rolling then long mountain canyon climb. Very difficult.

Riding Time/Speed Assumption (Without Stops): About 6 hours at 12 mph.

Start/End Point: South end of Broadway at Greenbriar Rd.

Best In Town/Path Ride to the Start: Marshall Route #6.

Directions: While the most direct route to Golden from Boulder is to travel straight south on Colo. 93, we highly recommend against biking on Colo. 93 between Colo. 128 and Golden. The traffic is very heavy, there are no shoulders and the traffic is traveling at very high speeds. Consequently, we recommend staying east on the Morgul-Bismark route to start, then over to Indiana Boulevard on the east side of Rocky Flats. To get specific:

Ride south to Marshall on the bike path/road or Colo. 93. (1.2 m.)

⌐ *Turn left (east) on Marshall Road (Colo. 170).* If you are on 93, there is a stop light at Colo. 170. If you take the path/side road bear right at the intersection in the group of houses, then left to the intersection with Marshall Road (Colo. 170). In either case, ride east on 170 and curve south at US36 to the road end intersection with McCaslin Boulevard. (3.8 m.)

⌐ *Turn right (south) at the stop sign onto McCaslin Blvd.*and ride to the road end at Colo. 128. (3.5 m.)

⌐ *Turn left (east) onto Colo. 128* to Indiana Boulevard. (.3 m.)

⌐ *Turn right (south) onto Indiana Blvd.* past the east entrance of Rocky Flats to stop sign at Colo. 72. (4.2 m.)

⌐ *Turn left (south) to remain on Indiana Blvd.* at the intersection with 72. Ride south to the turn off to Leyden at W. 82nd Ave. (0.4 m)

⌐ *Turn right (west) on W. 82nd Ave.* to Quacker Road. (1.1 m)

⌐ *Turn left (south) on Quacker Road* to 64th Ave. (2.3 m.)

⌐ *Turn right (west) on 64th* to Easley Road. (0.5 m.)

⌐ *Turn left (south) on Easley Road* to 60th. (0.5 m.)

⌐ *Turn right (west) on 60th* (turns into 58th) to Colo. 93. (1.9 m.)

⌐ *Turn left (south) on Colo. 93* to Golden Gate Canyon Rd. (2.2 m.)

⌐ *Turn right (west) on Golden Gate Canyon Road* up to the Park Visitor's Center (12.8 m.)

Refueling Possibilities: There are no refueling spots on the route. The closest diversion to food is to ride from the Visitor's Center 4.5 miles west on Golden Gate Canyon Rd. to the KOA Campground.

Additional Comments: Many will prefer to do the loop below to Colo. 119 but due to the heavy traffic caused by the gambling towns it has become less attractive. Wider shoulders on this stretch of 119 has lessened the impact of the increased traffic to a certain extent. Lack of shoulders and heavy weekend traffic in Golden Gate Canyon make weekdays and very early weekend days the best time to ride this route. It may be best to drive up to the corner of Colo. 72 and Indiana Blvd. to do the loop down Coal Creek Canyon or to Golden Gate Canyon Rd. & Colo. 93 to do the up and back.

Skinny Tire Variations:

S1. Golden or Arvada-From Quacker Rd. & 64th, turn left, east on 64th 1/2 mile to McIntyre Rd. Turn right (south) on McIntyre and ride to its end at 32nd St. Turn right (west) to go into Golden or left (east) to go towards Arvada.

S1a. Connection to Denver area's South Platte River trail system-It is possible to connect to the South Platte River Trail system of bike trails in 2 places in this part of town (see S1). The first is just south of the corner of Indiana St. and 72nd Ave. where Ralston Creek crosses Indiana. This trail travels east, merges with Clear Creek trail and eventually connects to the south Platte River Trail. Portions of this trail are still under construction as of this printing but are planned to be completed in 1995 or 1996.

The second option is to continue south on McIntyre (see S1 above) to just south of Colo. 58 where Clear Creek crosses. The Clear Creek trail follows the river east toward Denver and west into Golden. Again, parts of this trail are under construction but the section toward the east from Youngfield St. to the intersection with Ralston Creek is complete.

Please see the Ft. Lupton/Denver/South Platte River system for more details on possibilities once on this system of trails. (Route #19 Option S3)

S2. Loop back via Colo. 119/Coal Creek. Continue west on Golden Gate Canyon Rd. to Colo. 119. (5 miles) Turn right (north) on 119 to Colo. 72.(10 miles) Turn right (east) on 72 and continue up and over Wondervu down across Colo. 93 to Indiana Blvd. Turn left (north) and return via the main route. Please see Additional Comments above.(85 miles and 9,300 feet in climbing-50 miles from Indiana & Colo. 72)

S3. Lookout Mountain. From the corner of Colo. 93 and Golden Gate Canyon, continue south on 93 instead of turning on to Golden Gate Canyon Rd. to US 6. Cross US 6 and continue south about a mile to 19th St. Turn right (west) on 19th St. Ride through the homes and the Rock Gates then ascend the mountain about 5 miles and about 1,500 feet to Buffalo Bill's Grave.

Fat Tire Possibilities:

F1. Crawford Gulch-On the ascent of Golden Gate Canyon, about 4 miles above Colo. 93, is a gravel road that loops to the east of the main road and reconnects at the Park Visitor Center at Golden Gate Canyon Rd. In reverse, from the Visitor's Center ride east on County Rd. 57 on pavement about 4 miles to the exit from the park. Climb on gravel about 1,000 feet in several miles and then descend to Golden Gate Canyon Rd.

Allenspark via St. Vrain Canyon
Avoiding US 36
78 miles round trip and 4,700 feet of climbing

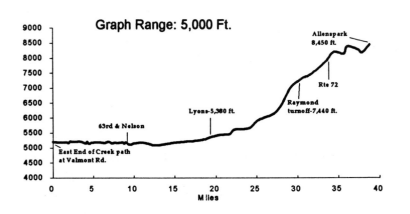

Hwy 66 to Longmont

75th St.

Diagonal Hwy (Colo. 119)

E. end of
Creek path
at Valmont

Hwy 66

Nelson Rd.

63rd St.

61st St.

Valmont Rd.

US 36 to
Boulder

Lyons F
S1

US 36 to
Estes Park

BOULDER

Colo. 7
S. St. Vrain
Canyon

F
Raymond/Riverside
S2

Peak to Peak
Hwy 72 to Ward
and Nederland
S4 & F1

Colo. 7 to
Estes Park
S3

Allenspark   F2

Graph Range: 5,000 Ft.

Main Route
23. ALLENSPARK via ST. VRAIN CANYON
avoiding US 36

Special Note: Due to the lack of shoulders, curves and heavy traffic north of Nelson Rd. on US 36 we suggest using 75th St. through Hygiene. As of this printing, US 36 is scheduled to be widened in 1997. After widening, US 36 should be safer.

Mileage(up and back): 78 Miles
Total Altitude Gain: 4,700 Feet
Steepness: The average grade from Lyons to Allenspark is 3.2% and fairly consistent. The steepest portion is near Colo. 72/Raymond where 5.2% grade is sustained for about 2.5 miles.
Traffic Volume/Existence of Shoulders: Low to moderate traffic and few shoulders on the plains. No shoulders in St. Vrain Canyon but low traffic volume. Wide shoulders after intersection with Colo. 7 with medium traffic.
Type/Difficulty: Rolling plains then steady, fairly steep climb. Very difficult.
Riding Time/Speed Assumption (Without Stops): Up-almost 5 hours at 8 mph. Down-3 hours 15 mph. Total riding time: 8 hours.
Start/End Point: East end of Boulder Creek Bike Path at about 55th and Valmont Road.
Best In Town/Path Ride to the Start: Boulder Creek Path Route # 7-east end.
Directions: Ride east on Valmont to 61st. (.8 m.)

⌐ *Turn left (north) on 61st,* which jogs over to become 63rd, until it dead ends into Nelson Road. (8.6 m.)

⌐ *Turn right (east) on Nelson Road* to 65th. (.3 m)

⌐ *Turn left (north) on 65th* which dead ends into St. Vrain. (1.5 m.)

⌐ *Turn right (east) on St. Vrain Road* to 75th. (1.3 m.)

⌐ *Turn left (north) on 75th* through Hygiene to Colo. 66. (1.9 m.)

⌐ *Turn left (west) on Colo. 66* and continue through Lyons. (5.4 m.)

⌐ *Turn left (south) on Colo. 7* where US 36 turns north at the light at the west end of Lyons. Stay on 7 until you get to the Allenspark/Ferncliff turnoff. (18.1 m.)

⌐ *Turn left (west) at the Ferncliff turnoff* and follow the road through Ferncliff up to Allenspark. It is more fun to return via Colo. 7 on the north end of Allenspark due to the straight, smooth and very fast descent. (.9 m.)

Refueling Possibilities: Hygiene. Lyons. There is a juice stand in the summer at the glacier overlook. If you detour through Raymond, there is a general store at the corner where you turn right to return to Colo. 7. A spring of very cold and clear water is available to the public on the left hand side of the road at the southeast end of Allenspark. There is a store in Ferncliff and a couple of restaurants in Allenspark. There is also a tourist shop with refreshments on Colo. 7 just to the north of the northern-most Allenspark turnoff.

Additional Comments: The best canyon ride in the county! Low traffic and great scenery make for an enjoyable but hard working ride. The descent can be great fun due to good pavement and lack of sharp curves.

Skinny Tire Variations:

S1. Drive to Lyons. Total up and back-38 miles and 3,700 feet in altitude. Closer to 4 hours total time.

S2. Raymond/Connect to Peak to Peak Hwy. Turn left into Riverside at mile 31.6, continue on to Raymond then right at the store back up to Colo. 7. The pavement is lower quality but it is a pleasant detour, or continue straight through Raymond to Colo. 72 at a point about 3 miles south of where Colo. 72 ends at Colo. 7.

S3. Estes Park. Head north on Colo. 7 out of Allenspark about 16 miles to Estes Park. See route #25 for Estes Park details.

S4. Ward Loop. Turn south on Colo. 72 to Ward and descend down Left Hand Canyon and back to Lyons or Boulder. (Loop is 65 miles and 4,800 feet in climbing.)

Fat Tire Possibilities:

F1. Peak to Peak Gravel Roads. Turn south on Colo. 72. Several gravel roads lead down to the east. (See Peak to Peak Highway route #14 for details).

F2. West from Allenspark there is a gravel forest access that goes to the National Park Boundary.

Mega Routes
Brief descriptions of very long routes

24. Fort Collins
25. Estes Park
26. Grand Loop

Mega Route
24. Fort Collins

Mileage(out and back): 80 miles
Total Altitude Gain: 2,500 feet
Traffic Volume/Existence of Shoulders: Varies.
Type/Difficulty: Long rolling ride.
Riding Time/Speed Assumption (Without Stops): 7 hours at about 12 mph.
Start/End Point: East end of Creek Path at 55th & Valmont.
Best In Town/Path Ride to the Start: Boulder Creek Path Route # 7-east end.
Directions: Follow directions for Carter Lake (route #20) to the Carter Lake Rd. turnoff. Continue north past Carter Lake Rd. on 23 Rd. to the dead end at 14 Rd. Turn right (east) on 14 Rd. to 21 Rd. (.8 mile). Turn left (north) on 21 Rd. to past Boedecker Lake to 20 Rd.(W 1st St.). Turn right (east) on 20 Rd. 1/2 mile to Wilson Ave. Turn left (north) on Wilson Ave. across US 34 and through Loveland to Ft. Collins (the road changes names as you go but you will end up at the south west corner of town at about Taft & Harmony)
Refueling Possibilities: Hygiene, Loveland, Ft. Collins.
Additional Comments:
Skinny Tire Variations:

     S1. Masonville Loop-Just to the north of Harmony St.in Ft. Collins on the left (west) is a stop light at 38E Rd. Turn left (west) on 38E Rd. This goes to Masonville. (9.4 miles). Follow 27 Rd. south to US 34. You now have 2 choices. You may avoid a long distance on US 34 by turning right (west) on US 34 for less than a mile to 29 Rd. Turn left (south) on 29 Rd. to 20 Rd. on the left and join the S1 variation in the Carter Lake Route #20.

Mega-Route
25. Estes Park Loop

Mileage(loop): 115 miles
Total Altitude Gain: 6,500 feet
Steepness: The grade on Devil's Gulch Road averages just over 4% from US 34 to Estes Park but a short section above Glen Haven of about .25 mile is over 10%.
Traffic Volume/Existence of Shoulders: US 34 can be very busy. Minimal shoulders. See Main Routes of Carter Lake, Peak to Peak & Ward for details.
Type/Difficulty: Brutal mountain ride.
Riding Time/Speed Assumption (Without Stops): 10 hours at 11.5 mph.
Start/End Point: East end of Boulder Creek Path about 55th & Valmont.
Best In Town/Path Ride to the Start: Boulder Creek Path Route # 7-east end.
Directions: Follow Carter Lake Main Route #20, then Pole Hill variation S1 to 29 Rd. and continue north to US 34. Turn left (west) on US 34 and follow about 10 miles to Devil's Gulch Rd. (To Glen Haven). Turn right (north) onto Devil's Gulch Rd. and follow in to US 34 near the town of Estes Park. Turn left (east) on US 34 to the junction of US 36. Take US 36 east to the junction with Colo. 7. Turn right (south) on Colo. 7 and climb out of the Estes Park valley and beyond for 16 miles to Colo. 72 just past (south of) Allenspark. Turn right (south) on Colo. 72 to Ward. Turn left into Ward and descend Left Hand Canyon (See Ward Main Route #18) for further details.
Refueling Possibilities: Carter Lake (north end), several restaurants on US 34, Estes Park, Ward
Additional Comments: US 34 can be very busy with RV's. The ascent of US 34 is best done early in the day.
Skinny Tire Variations:

    S1. St. Vrain Canyon Descent. Stay on Colo 7 and descend to Lyons. See Allenspark Route #23 for details. The mileage differs liitle from the main route but you do avoid about 1,500 feet of climbing.

    S2. Coal Creek Canyon Descent From Ward, continue south on Colo. 72 through Pinecliffe & Wondervu for a truly grueling 142 mile, 8,500 feet of climbing, day.
Fat Tire Possibilities: See main routes in this area.

Mega-Route
26. Grand Loop

Mileage(loop): 220 miles

Total Altitude Gain: Approx. 11,000

Traffic Volume/Existence of Shoulders: Varies but the greatest chance for the worst conditions (no shoulder and heavy traffic) are mid-Summer weekends on Trailridge Road.

Type/Difficulty: Extremely difficult mountain ride.

Riding Time/Speed Assumption: 2 to 4 days (it can be done in 1 day).

Start/End Point: Boulder

Directions: (Very Generally) Follow directions for Ward route #18 or Allenspark route # 23; then ride north to Estes Park or follow Estes Park route #25. Enter Rocky Mtn. Nat. Park at the south entrance (US 36) and follow Trail Ridge Road (US 34) to Granby. Turn south on US 40 in Granby to I-70. Turn east on the I-70 frontage road to Lookout Mtn. Road. Follow this northeast to Golden. Avoid Colo. 93 by riding east through Golden on 32nd Ave. to McIntyre St. Turn north on McIntyre and follow it to its dead end into 64th Ave. See the Golden Gate Park route #22 for details for getting back to Boulder.

Additional Comments: Obviously, this is a brief description of this route. If you plan such an endeavor you should be in top condition, know what you are in for and plan the trip carefully. This description is merely food for thought.

Skinny Tire Variations: Steamboat Springs? Salt Lake City? Seattle?

Summary of some of the more significant Colorado Bicycling Laws

(Local ordinance can be more restrictive but not less so. Please see Boulder's variations at the end of this section.)

Where may you bike? Any public right-of-way that is not prohibited by signage or not forbidden by law. (The only restricted 2-lane roads of which we are aware within reasonable biking distance of Boulder are: Clear Creek Canyon-US 6 between Golden & I-70 near Idaho Springs, and I-25).

Rights & Responsibilities. A bicyclist has all the rights and responsibilities of any driver of any other vehicle except when specifically regulated by law or when certain regulations, by their nature, cannot apply to bicycles. Municipalities may add further restrictions beyond those in the state law by passing local ordinances. It is your responsibility to know the law of the municipality in which you are bicycling. (That's why Boulder's Ordinances are listed below).

Bicyclists who violate the traffic laws are subject to **the same penalties as drivers of motor vehicles**, except that no penalty points shall be assessed against the cyclist's driver's license.

If a bicyclist is stopped for a traffic violation and the officer has reason to believe that the bicyclist will not appear in court or the officer is unsure of the bicyclist's identity, the officer may arrest the bicyclist and require the bicyclist to post bond. **(So, for this reason and in case you get hurt, bring ID when you cycle).**

Operation of Bicycles

You **MUST**:
-Ride in the **right lane** except:
      -when overtaking another bicycle or other vehicle proceeding in the same direction.
      -when preparing for a left turn.
      -when necessary to avoid hazardous conditions.
-Ride as **close to the right side of the right lane** as is practicable when being overtaken by another vehicle.
-Ride **on the paved shoulder** whenever a paved shoulder suitable for bicycle riding is present.

-Ride **single file** on the roadway if motor vehicle traffic is approaching within 300 feet from the rear or if sight distance is limited within 300 feet in front or behind you.
-Ride within a single lane if you are riding two abreast.
-Keep at least **one hand on the handlebars** at all times.
-Obey all traffic signs & signals.
-**Signal** your intention to turn, slow, or stop. When turning, you must signal continuously at least 100 feet before the turn and while **stopped**, waiting to turn, unless use of your hand is needed
-Ride to the right, **with** the flow of traffic.

You **MAY:**
-Ride two abreast on the roadway if there are no motor vehicles approaching from the rear within 300 feet and if there are no sight obstructions within 300 feet in front of or behind you.
-Ride two abreast on paths or bicycle lanes.
-Ride more than two abreast on the shoulder if all cyclists are completely on the shoulder.

You are **NOT ALLOWED** to:
-Carry more people at one time on the bicycle than the number for which your bicycle is designed or equipped.
-**Attach** yourself or your bicycle to any motor vehicle on a roadway.
-Wear **headphones** while on a roadway.

Riding on **Sidewalks** & in **Crosswalks**
-You are not allowed to ride on a sidewalk or in a crosswalk where it is prohibited by signs or ordinances.
-While on a sidewalk or in a crosswalk you must yield the right-of-way to any pedestrians, and give an audible signal before overtaking or passing them.
-If you are riding or walking your bicycle in a crosswalk or on a sidewalk you have all the rights and duties applicable to a pedestrian under the same circumstances.

Equipment-From sundown to sunup or when weather or other conditions cause poor visibility, your bicycle must be equipped with a **rear red reflector** and reflectors on both sides. Both mustbe able to be seen for 600 feet in a car's headlamps. You must also have a white front **headlight** that can be seen for at least 500 feet from the front of your bicycle.

Your bicycle must be equipped with a working brake or **brakes** that will enable you to stop within 25 feet from the speed of 10 mph on dry, level, clean pavement.

Harassment and Reckless Endangerment of a Bicyclist

Harassment is a misdemeanor offense and may include threats, taunting, or intimidation. Reckless endangerment is also a misdemeanor offense and involves conduct which places another person at risk of personal injury. In both situations the police should be notified and given information such as vehicle and driver description along with location, date, time, and witnesses.

All of the above is from The Colorado Bicycle Manual published by Colorado Bicycle Program June, 1994 which is a summary. **There are more laws which apply to bicycles. Please contact the Colorado Bicycle Program for a more complete listing.**

A summary of some of BOULDER'S significant FURTHER DEFINITIONS/RESTRICTIONS

Boulder's City Ordinances define how far to the right you must ride. They say that you **must ride in the right 4 feet of the roadway**, except when reasonably necessary for safety or when you do not impede traffic. You may **move to the center of the lane** when:

-Approaching an intersection.
-Riding next to parked cars, and then within 4 feet of the parked cars.
-Avoiding obstacles or hazards.
--**Riding at the same speed as traffic, such as downhill or in slow traffic.**

Motorists in the City of Boulder **must allow at least THREE feet of clearance** or must change lanes if the lane is too narrow to pass.

In **stopped or slow traffic, bicyclists may pass on the right**, but may not pass a moving vehicle signaling a right turn.

Summarized from a GO Boulder publication (June 1993) from the City of Boulder.

Please contact GO Boulder for a more complete list of ordinances affecting bicyclists.

It's not the law but it's a great idea-Wear a helmet whenever on a bike.

Scoring your ride by the Struthers Method.

I don't know about you but when I get home from a ride and someone asks "How was your ride?", I might reply "Great weather, not enough miles; but when that old guy on a new Klein blew by me it really ruined my day!" or "Kind of windy but I passed 4 people on the climb and they were all younger than me so that part was great". Not that I'm the competitive sort, mind you but, let's be honest, those things can affect the way you feel about your ride. So I've developed a shorthand way to respond to that question of how the ride went. I can now say "It was a 50 pointer". Much more succinct–don't you think? And you can accumulate your points over a month or season! "I had an 800 point month, how was yours?" Remember, if you can't assign a number to it, it can't be recorded and accumulated. If it can't be recorded or accumulated, the accountants will tell you that it didn't really happen at all. No matter how much training you do, if you don't score it, your riding may be all for naught!

We all know that mileage is the touchstone for cyclists measuring their year, month or ride. What caused me to start thinking about a better method for measuring my rides was riding in the mountains. I knew my 35 mile ride up in the mountains was much better training than a 50 mile flat ride. During a long van ride to a cycling trip, I offered my opinion to my fellow cyclists that every 1,000 feet of altitude climbed was worth an additional 10 miles of riding, from an effort perspective. They responded: "But what about a head wind on the flat ride.", "And what about the weight of the rider and the bike", "And doesn't the grade matter?", "What about the relative position of celestial bodies?" And on and on for hours. Yea, Yea, Yea. So it ain't perfect. but it's close.

The Base Model is for the non-competitive riders (both of us) and the competitive model is for the rest of you. In order for the Competitive Model to work well, though, you need to be on a route with a fair number of other cyclists. If you aren't, then default back to the Base Model. It also helps to ride your old Schwinn Varsity in your cut-off jeans and t-shirt when going for maximum points under the Competitive Model. Of course, a can of spray paint and the right decals can be very deceptive, if you know what I mean. But we're operating on the honor system here, right? Feel free to adapt the model to your riding conditions but remember we are all subject to audit in the end.

Scoring your Ride-The Base Model

100 points maximum

Distance: Maximum 20 points. 1 point for every 5 miles you ride that day.

Altitude: Maximum-20 points. 1 point for every 500 feet you climb that day. If you live or ride on the flats, you may ignore the altitude component and change the maximum for distance up to 40 points.

How you Feel: 20 points maximum.

	Points Scored
Resting Heart Rate=0 after the ride	0
In the Hospital, didn't finish the ride	2
In the Hospital, but finished the ride	4
Hurled on your new Kestrel headset	6
Almost hurled on your new headset	8
Legs hurt, lungs hurt but made it	10
Legs hurt OR Lungs hurt-not both!	12
Dragged on in	14
Felt OK but glad to not have gone farther	16
Felt good and could have ridden farther	18
Felt great and could do it all over again	20

Weather: 10 point maximum

Raining or snowing and windy and cold	2
2 of 3-precipitation/windy/cold	4
1 of 3-precipitation/windy/cold	6
HOT & Sunny	8
Cool, no wind, no rain-great day	10

Equipment: 10 points

Didn't finish ride due to equipment failure	2
Finished ride but spent more time fixing than riding	4
Had to stop more than once due to equipment (includes flats)	6
Had to stop or were delayed in starting due to equipment	8
No Problems	10

Relationship with Motorized Vehicles: 10 points

Didn't finish ride due to contact with MV	0
Had contact with MV but finished ride	2
More than one Close Encounter	4
Only one Close Encounter	6
Lots of traffic but no Close Encounters	8
Little traffic and no Close Encounters	10

Fuel: 10 points

Bonked-Didn't finish ride	0
Bonked-Finished ride	2
Ran out of food and water	4
Ran out of food or water	6
Took lots of food and water-came back with most or all of it	8
Took lots of food and water-had a little of both left	10

Scoring your Ride-The Competitive Model

100 points maximum (This model works best for the competitive person when riding a route where you encounter many other riders but may not work well when riding in a pack). The scoring is the same as above in Distance and Altitude but cut the points in the rest of the categories in half, both in maximum and item scores. Now add the following category. You should still have a maximum of 100 points.

How you rode in relationship to other cyclists-30 points maximum

Assumption: You are riding alone-not drafting in a pack.
Did you pass more people than passed you? If yes, 10 points
For each person you passed that you can answer yes to the following questions: 1 point/person (10 point maximum for each category-pick the 10 where you can score!)

Age (10 points max.) Were they younger than you?
Equipment (10 points max.) Did they have a more expensive bike and clothing or were they wearing a local team's racing jersey or were they on a road bike and you on a mountain bike?